CARO

AT THE NATIONAL GALLERY

SCULPTURE FROM PAINTING

John Golding

NATIONAL GALLERY PUBLICATIONS, LONDON

This book was published to
accompany an exhibition at
The National Gallery, London
25 February – 4 May 1998

Supported by The Bernard Sunley
Charitable Foundation and
The Henry Moore Foundation

First published in Great Britain in 1998 by
National Gallery Publications Limited
5/6 Pall Mall East, London SW1Y 5BA

ISBN 1 85709 221 X paperback
525272
British Library Cataloguing-in-Publication
Data. A catalogue record is available from
the British Library.

EDITOR Felicity Luard
ASSISTANT EDITOR John Jervis
DESIGNER Sara Robin

Printed and bound in Great Britain
by Scanplus, London

FRONT COVER
Anthony Caro
Arena Piece, 'Beginning'
1995 (fig. 54)

BACK COVER
Giotto
Madonna in Majesty
*c.*1306–10 (fig. 53)

CONTENTS

FOREWORD

A strange idea, you might think, to show sculptures at the National Gallery, a collection which famously has no three-dimensional works of art. But the pieces in question are by Anthony Caro, who for many years now has been producing sculpted meditations on European paintings from Giotto to Matisse, revisiting Rembrandt's *Descent from the Cross*, Goya's *Third of May, 1808*, and Manet's *Le Déjeuner sur l'herbe*, exploring and transforming the ways by which these images achieve their aims, forging (almost literally) an alternative means to the same final pathos, and sharpening our perception of both in the process.

A few years ago the National Gallery asked Anthony Caro if he would consider making a sculpture related to a picture in the Collection. The result was not one work, but five variations on Van Gogh's *Chair*. Caro's materials are as wilfully humdrum as those that make up the chair itself, and his surfaces, perhaps paradoxically, less immediate renderings of wood and straw than Van Gogh's own. Caro's great strength has always been space; and he has constructed and constricted the space in which the chair is set until it becomes itself a subject, a profound, disconcerting analogue of the planes in the painting, space retreating into panic. A new work of art has been made, and Van Gogh's picture rescued from the dulling of a false familiarity which is the greatest danger famous paintings must endure.

If our thanks are due first to Anthony Caro for so generously responding to our invitation, we owe a further debt of gratitude to John Golding whose essay eloquently sets the *Chairs* in the context of Caro's career, to the lenders to the exhibition, to Ian Barker of Annely Juda Fine Art, to The Henry Moore Foundation, and to The Bernard Sunley Charitable Foundation, which has once again allowed the public to look at a part of the Collection in a new light.

Neil MacGregor DIRECTOR

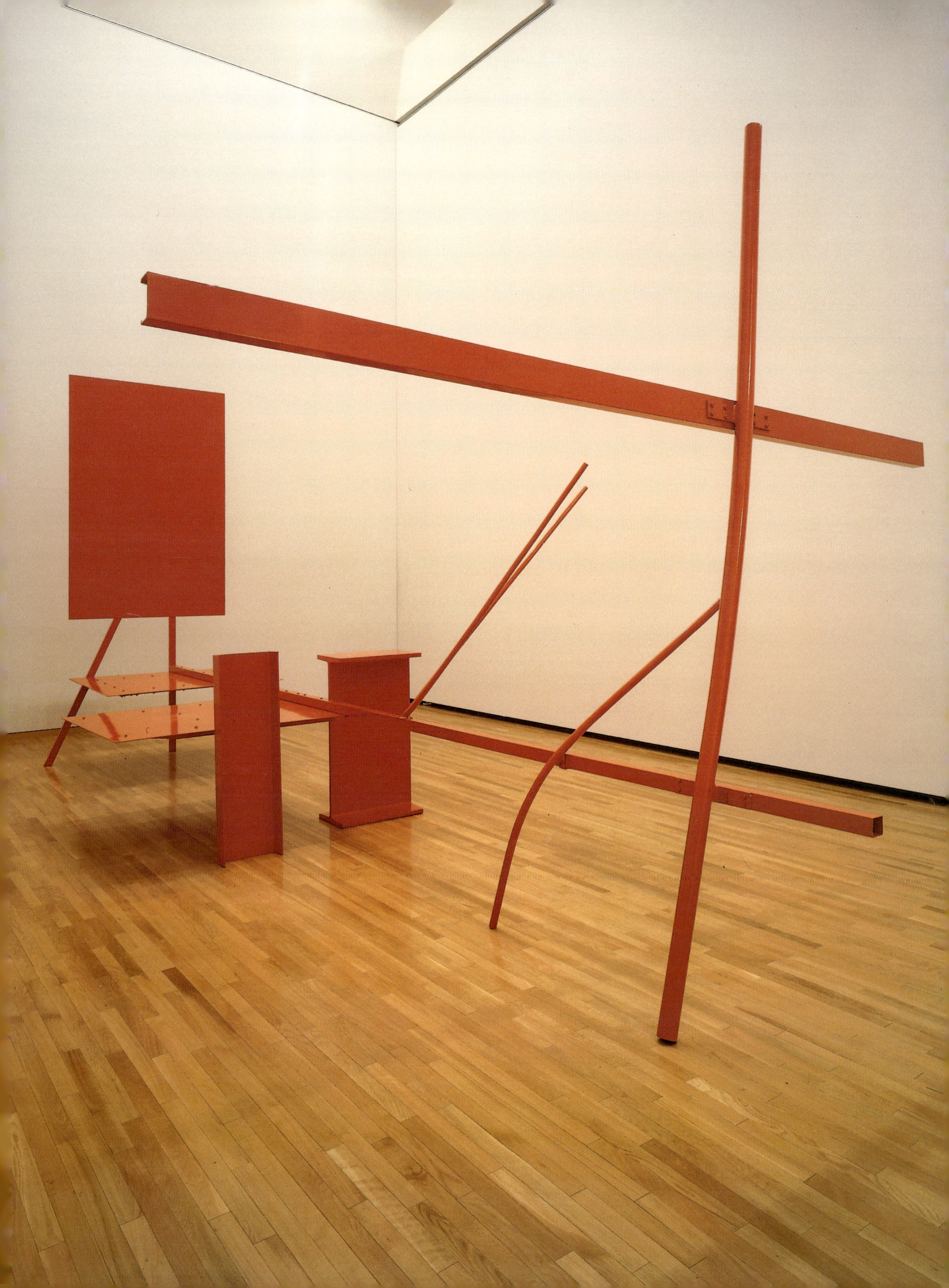

ANTHONY CARO AND PAINTING

WORKING WITH THE MASTERS

The bringing together of a high proportion of Anthony Caro's sculptures executed after paintings by masters of the past celebrates something unique in the annals of art. As sister arts, painting and sculpture have always complemented and nourished each other. There is evidence to suggest that in classical antiquity painting coexisted with sculpture in a symbiotic relationship. It had been so in the greatest phases of Egyptian art, and it is something we witness particularly vividly in the art of the Italian Renaissance. To mention only one connection directly relevant to Caro: Mantegna, whom he was to paraphrase, was deeply aware of the achievements of Donatello in Padua. To this day Donatello remains the sculptor of the past dearest to Caro's heart. Closer to us in time, Henry Moore, with whom Caro served a two-year apprenticeship as a part-time assistant, executed plaster maquettes (fig. 3) from his own small Cézanne *Three Bathers* of about 1875 (fig. 2), and the lessons that Moore learned from doing so were indirectly to inform his subsequent sculpture. But no sculptor has ever before transposed a wide range of pictorial masterpieces into three dimensions with a view to enriching the sculptural language of his own time. Another cardinal factor in assessing this venture: Caro is an abstract artist. Not only do these sculptures pay tribute to painting of the past in a different medium, but they also transform it into a different visual idiom. They constitute a new genre in art.

1 **ANTHONY CARO**
Early One Morning 1962
Steel and aluminium painted red
290 x 620 x 333 cm
LONDON, TATE GALLERY

Caro's sculpture acknowledged a debt to painting very early on, in the figure pieces of the mid-1950s which first brought him to critical attention. The voices of de Kooning, Bacon and Dubuffet informed the works shown at his first one-man exhibition held at the Gimpel Fils Gallery, London, in 1957. But a much more profound if less direct debt to contemporary painting is made manifest in the sculpture Caro executed on his return to London after his first historic visit to America in 1959 – referred to by himself as his 'conversion' – and in the works he executed on both sides of the Atlantic during the next two decades. Already, before leaving for the United States, Caro had met Clement Greenberg who was then establishing himself as the most important formalist art critic of his generation. At the time of their encounter Greenberg was about to publish his influential book of essays, *Art and Culture*. This ended with an analysis of Cubist *collage*. Earlier, in 1948, Greenberg had defined Cubism as 'the epoch-making feat of twentieth-century art, a style that has changed and determined the complexion of Western art as radically as Renaissance naturalism once did.'[1] Caro now became what he has described as a 'sculptural *collagiste*', intuitively assembling and welding together abstract sculptural elements to form cohesive, aesthetically compelling sculptural entities. In 1958 Greenberg revised an earlier essay, *The New Sculpture*, and claimed that, 'sculpture – that long eclipsed art – stands to gain by

BELOW LEFT
2 **PAUL CÉZANNE**
Three Bathers c.1875
Oil on canvas
28.8 x 31.2 cm
PRIVATE COLLECTION

BELOW RIGHT
3 **HENRY MOORE**
Three Bathers – After Cézanne 1978
Bronze, originally modelled in plaster
Length 30.5 cm
THE HENRY MOORE FOUNDATION

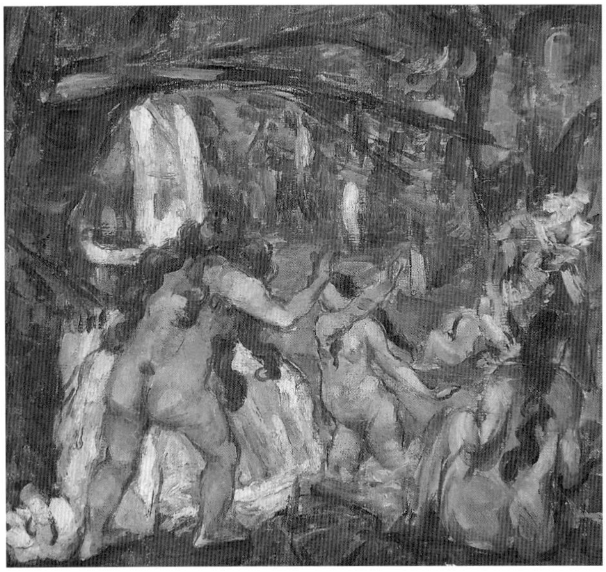

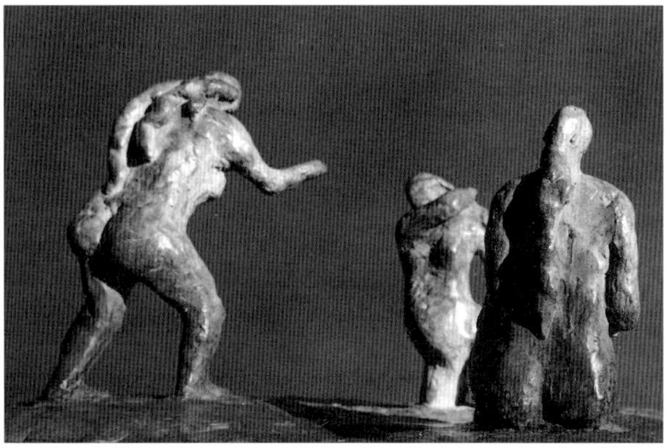

the modernist "reduction" as painting doesn't.'[2] Greenberg's views were conditioned by his admiration for the work of David Smith whom he had viewed as the leading sculpture of his generation. Now he was coming to see Caro not only as Smith's successor but also as a figure who personified the sculptural renaissance he had predicted.

Caro was to profit from Smith's example. Smith, who had worked for a spell as a riveter at a car factory, had opened up the horizons heralded by the welded sculptures of Picasso and Julio González, themselves 'sculptural *collagistes*'. Like Caro, Smith insisted that he 'belonged with painters'.[3] He had been trained as a painter. As a sculptor he sought to put his art into a wider context by referring back to painting, mostly to recent painting of a Surrealist persuasion. Caro proceeded in a totally different way. He recognised that developments in American painting were in advance of those in contemporary sculpture, precisely because painting had, in his own words, 'gone further along the road to abstraction'.[4] Above all, he turned to painting because as a sculptor it could stimulate him but give him 'no direct instructions'.[5] His ambition was to give to sculpture the openness, the breadth and freedom of innovation that he saw in the work of his new American painter friends such as Kenneth Noland, Jules Olitski and Helen Frankenthaler. He then sought out for himself the sculptural means by which to do so. Many of Smith's sculptures act as metaphors for the human body, a fact that he often acknowledged in his choice of titles (his *Sentinel* series for example). They evoke in the spectator a bodily response; we measure ourselves up to them as presences that relate to us in a visceral, physical way (fig. 5). This was something that Caro now sought to eliminate from his work; he wanted from his viewers a response only from the eye. He did so originally by getting rid of the traditional sculptural base or stand. He placed his works directly on the floor or ground so that they either thrust their way back and forth horizontally along it or seemed to float above it, suspended in space (fig. 4). These features were recognised immediately as being unique to Caro's art. As opposed to Smith, Caro distrusted Surrealism. The use of metaphor, so dear to the Surrealists, plays no part at all in his art; it never 'stands in' for something else and is always simply itself.

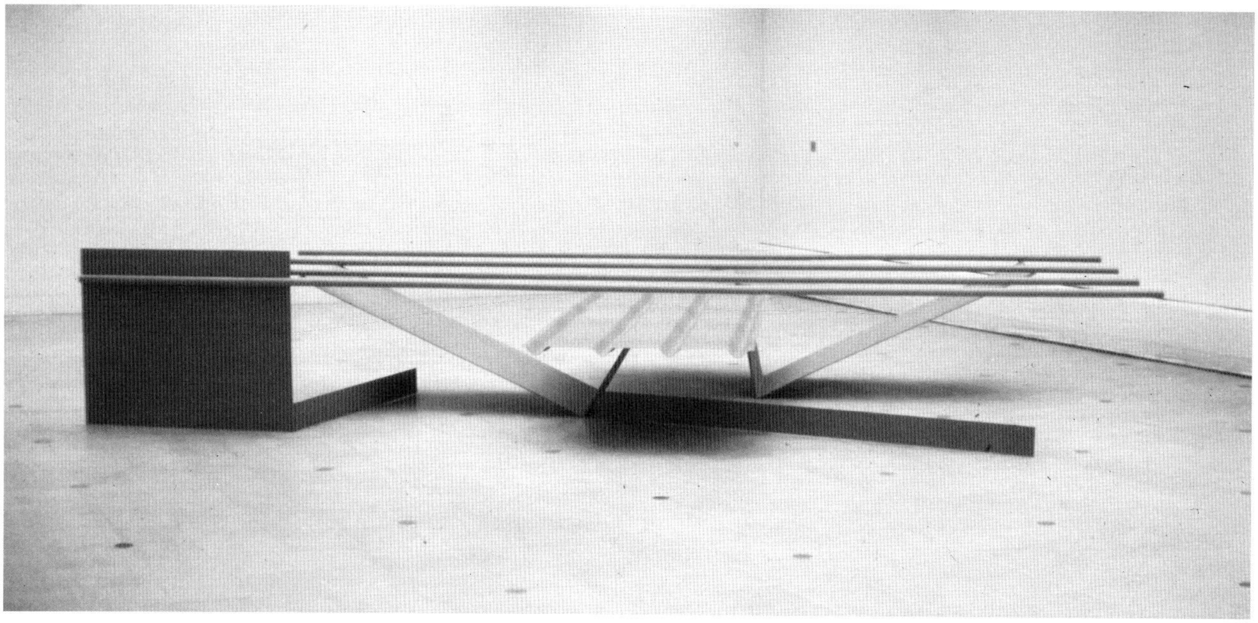

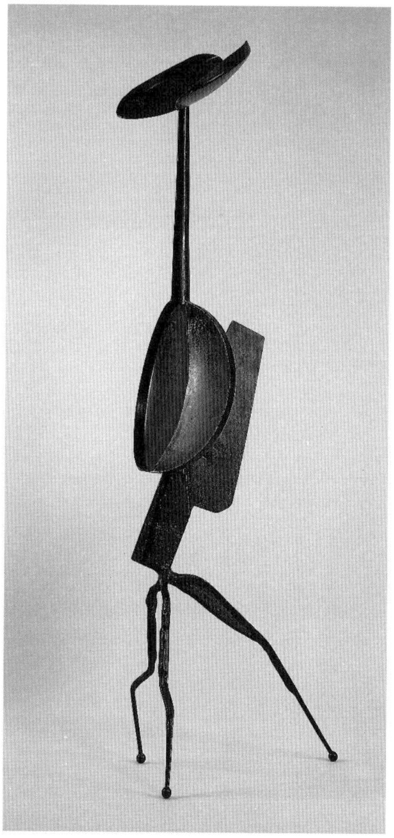

Caro is possibly the most prolific sculptor of his age and certainly the most inventive. Over the years his art has become increasingly rich and varied, and as he enters a fifth decade of productivity it becomes ever harder to generalise about his work. But many of the characteristics of the sculptures of his early maturity persist. Significantly enough these are qualities most often associated with pictorial art. And it is proof of Caro's innate sculptural genius that they are invariably put to sculptural, three-dimensional ends. To begin with, Caro's sculptures often have a strong sense of frontality, of having a front and back. This is already true of *Twenty Four Hours* of 1960 (fig. 7), the first of what artists would call his 'break-through' pieces; the circular, target-like form paid friendly tribute to Noland's current painting (fig. 6). The side views of Caro's sculptures are often the thinnest or tightest, but they can also be the most informative because they tell us how the works are put or held together, just as the back views often read as reversed and simplified diagrams for the more complex frontal elevations. And then no other sculptor has made such extensive use of flat, two-dimensional planes. As in painting these can enhance a sense of frontality, although in Caro's work they are most

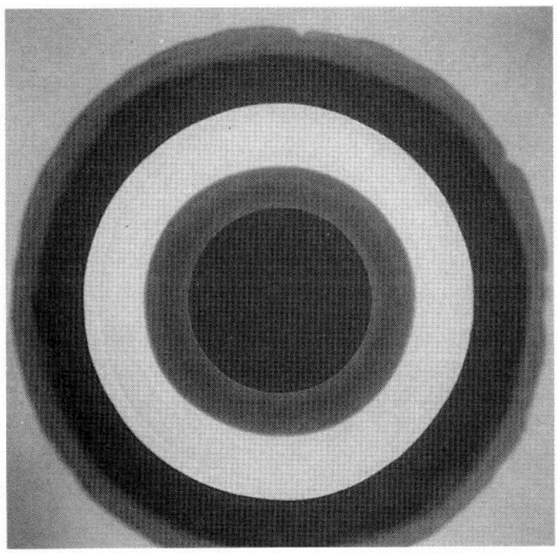

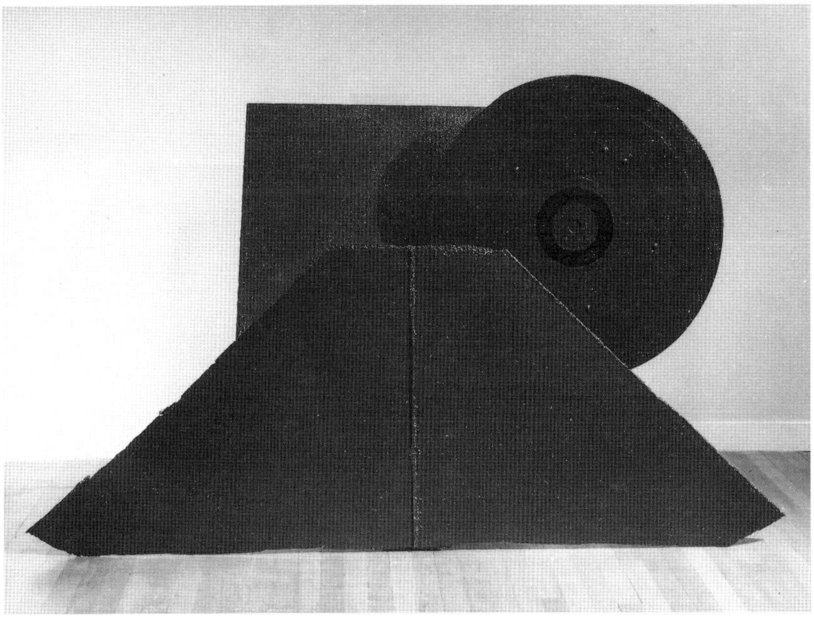

OPPOSITE ABOVE
4 **ANTHONY CARO**
Prairie 1967
Steel painted matt yellow
96.5 x 582 x 320 cm
WASHINGTON, NATIONAL GALLERY OF ART (on loan from Collection of Lois and Georges de Menil)

OPPOSITE BELOW
5 **DAVID SMITH**
Tanktotem III 1953
Steel
214.5 x 68.5 x 51 cm
TORONTO, COLLECTION OF MR AND MRS DAVID MIRVISH

ABOVE LEFT
6 **KENNETH NOLAND**
Bloom 1960
Acrylic on canvas
170 x 171 cm
DÜSSELDORF, KUNSTSAMMLUNG NORDRHEIN-WESTFALEN

ABOVE RIGHT
7 **ANTHONY CARO**
Twenty Four Hours 1960
Steel painted dark brown and black
138.4 x 223.5 x 83.8 cm
LONDON, TATE GALLERY

often subtly angled into depth, or, if placed more or less parallel to each other, they act as markers into space, defining its very properties. They do not displace space, as in traditional sculpture, but articulate and organise it before our eyes. The use of the flat upright plane as a primary sculptural element characterises, for example, *Early One Morning* of 1962 (fig. 1), a pivotal work of Caro's first artistic maturity.

David Smith makes frequent use of the flat plane, most notably in his *Cubi* series of the 1960s, but we are invariably aware of his planes as defining one face of a solid. Caro's flat planes speak only of themselves and to each other in sculptural dialogue. Often, and this can be seen once again in *Early One Morning*, they further communicate by the rhythms set up between them by slender upright or slightly tipped verticals, or by bent, curved, strip-like configurations – by a sculptor drawing through space in metal. Sometimes the two-dimensional plane is emptied out so that it becomes a window, recalling a painting's stretcher or its frame. In *The Window*, of 1966–7 (fig. 8), and related works, Caro makes use of flat planes of wire mesh, creating effects of transparency, dear to so much painting, but rare in sculpture. The *Straight* pieces of 1972 (fig. 9), which make use of irregular

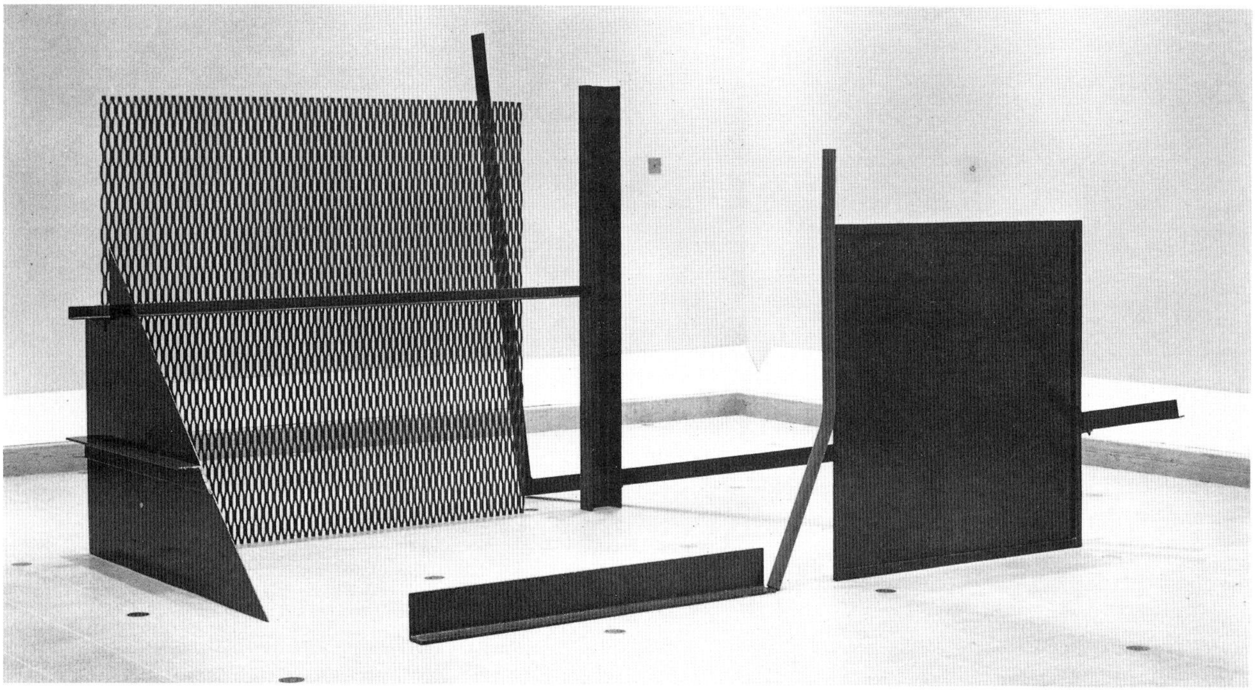

ABOVE
8 ANTHONY CARO
The Window 1966–7
Steel painted green and olive green
215 x 320.5 x 390 cm
LONDON, PRIVATE COLLECTION

RIGHT
9 ANTHONY CARO
Straight On 1972
Steel rusted with red paint rubbed in
201 x 173 x 132 cm
LONDON, PRIVATE COLLECTION

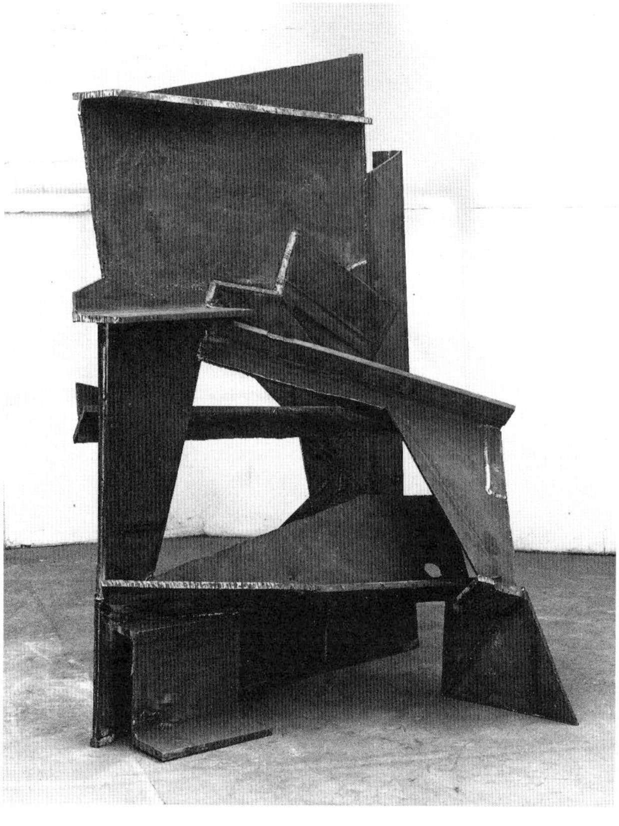

'windows', are mostly vertical in their orientation, and articulate space in ways analogous to those employed in Cubist painting. The sculptural as opposed to pictorial use of the two-dimensional plane is reinforced by the way in which it is deployed horizontally, in parallel layers. This, too, is a feature of *Early One Morning*. Almost all the sculptures of the 1960s were coloured, sometimes brightly, and most often in a single hue. But when in the early 1970s Caro decided to let metal, above all steel, speak for itself, texture and patina become increasingly important, a sculptor's substitute for painterly effects.

Although much of the greatest American abstract painting evokes analogies with landscape, sensations engendered by landscape find few echoes in Caro's sculpture, and at least until very recently he has preferred to have his works placed and seen in indoor settings. Yet his work has shown great sensitivity to place, to his surroundings, and above all to the different working conditions by which he has been challenged. The works executed at Veduggio in Italy and in Toronto during the first half of the 1970s, and the series produced in 1977, also in Canada, when he was artist in residence at the Emma Lake summer workshop run by the University of Saskatchewan, are totally different from each other in feeling, as are the works of the *Catalan* series executed a decade later. The soft-edged rolled steel, with its wavy, almost crumbly edges, which had caught Caro's eye at Veduggio's Ripamonte Factory (fig. 12), and which helped to characterise the sculptures he executed there, is painterly in its appeal. Significantly, while working abroad, opening up his art to new stimuli, pictorial analogies are frequently evoked, although these often draw on memories of pictorial effects stored and treasured in memory. At Veduggio Caro was struck and stimulated by the strong contrasts between dark and light experienced when coming in and out of his working spaces, and his awareness of the importance of sculptural silhouette was sharpened. This is reflected by the way in which large, rough, uneven, dark metallic shapes catch and define empty areas of light and space (fig. 10). The Veduggio pieces also have about them an architectural quality; forms are reminiscent of doorways, posts and lintels, embedded in fragments of wall. But they also evoke comparison with the open,

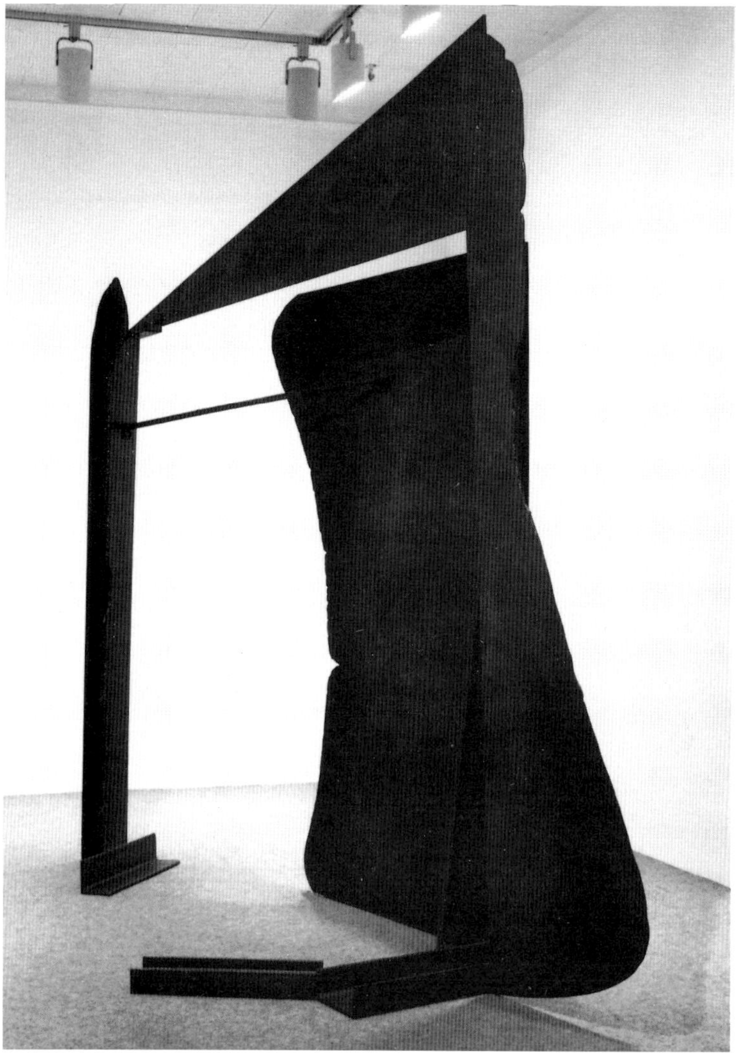

LEFT
10 **ANTHONY CARO**
Veduggio Sun 1972–3
Steel rusted and varnished
251.5 x 305 x 137 cm
DALLAS, MUSEUM OF FINE ARTS

BELOW
11 **HELEN FRANKENTHALER**
Orange Shapes in a Frame 1964–6
Acrylic on canvas
236 x 188 cm
WINNETKA, ILLINOIS, Collection of Mr and Mrs Robert B. Mayer

OPPOSITE
12 Anthony Caro at the Veduggio workshop, Italy, 1972

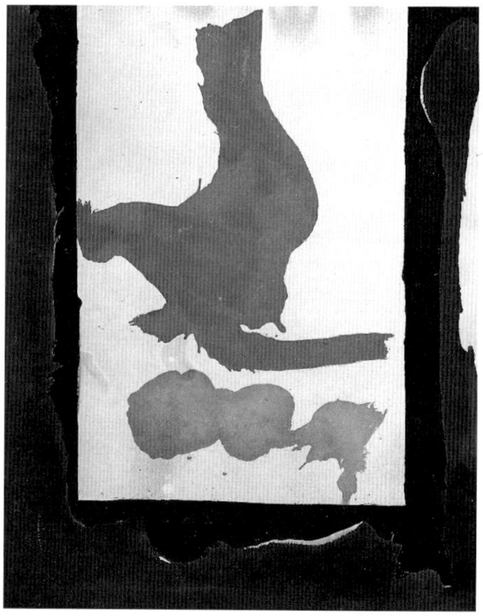

atmospheric, colouristic fields of Frankenthaler (fig. 11) and Olitski, held and caught in place by upright planes at the paintings' edges or internally articulated by bars or planes of denser paint.

Caro's working spell at the York Steel Company in Toronto, where he had the use of gantries and mobile cranes, allowed him to produce his largest and most monumental sculptures to date (fig. 13). Yet all the titles of these works include the word *Flat* or *Flats*, and their vast, towering and expanding forms produce, paradoxically, some of the most painterly of all Caro's sculptures, largely because of the way in which their softly undulating forms are pressed and flattened back into each other. The shapes, with their curving edges, evoke in steel sensations analogous to the diaphanous 'veil' paintings of Morris Louis (fig. 14) which Caro remembers discussing with his American painter friends. It is in the *York* series perhaps more than in any other of Caro's sculptures that we are made aware most strongly of the supreme importance played by the narrowed, trapped spaces contained between the monolithic vertical and gently reclining upright elements that first catch and hold the eye.

That Caro should at times have worked with the achievements of his painter friends in mind is only natural. But a work such as *Tundra* of 1975 (fig. 15), closely related to the *York* series, serves to

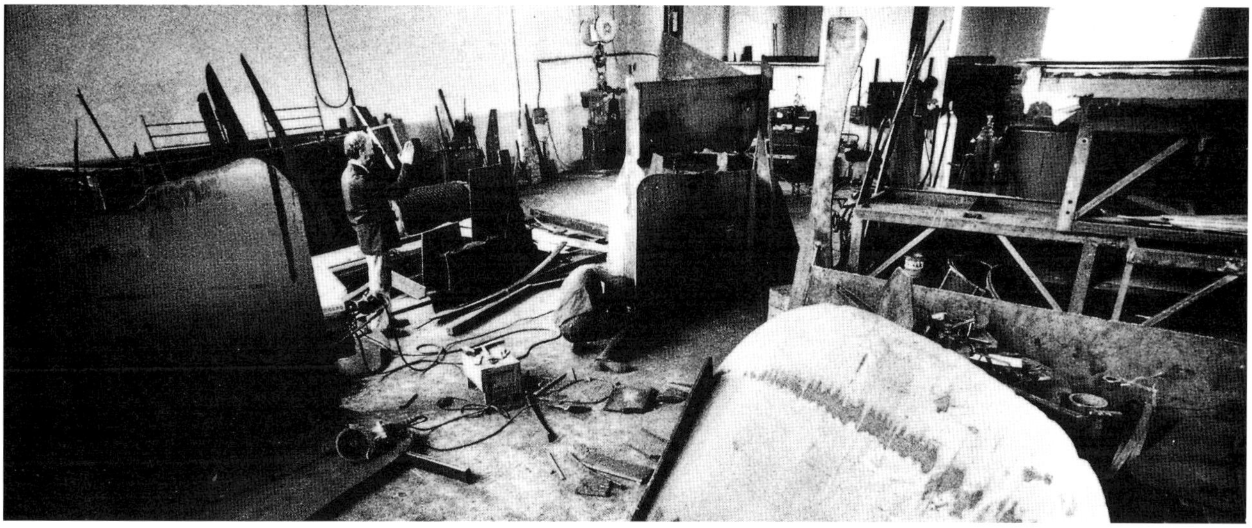

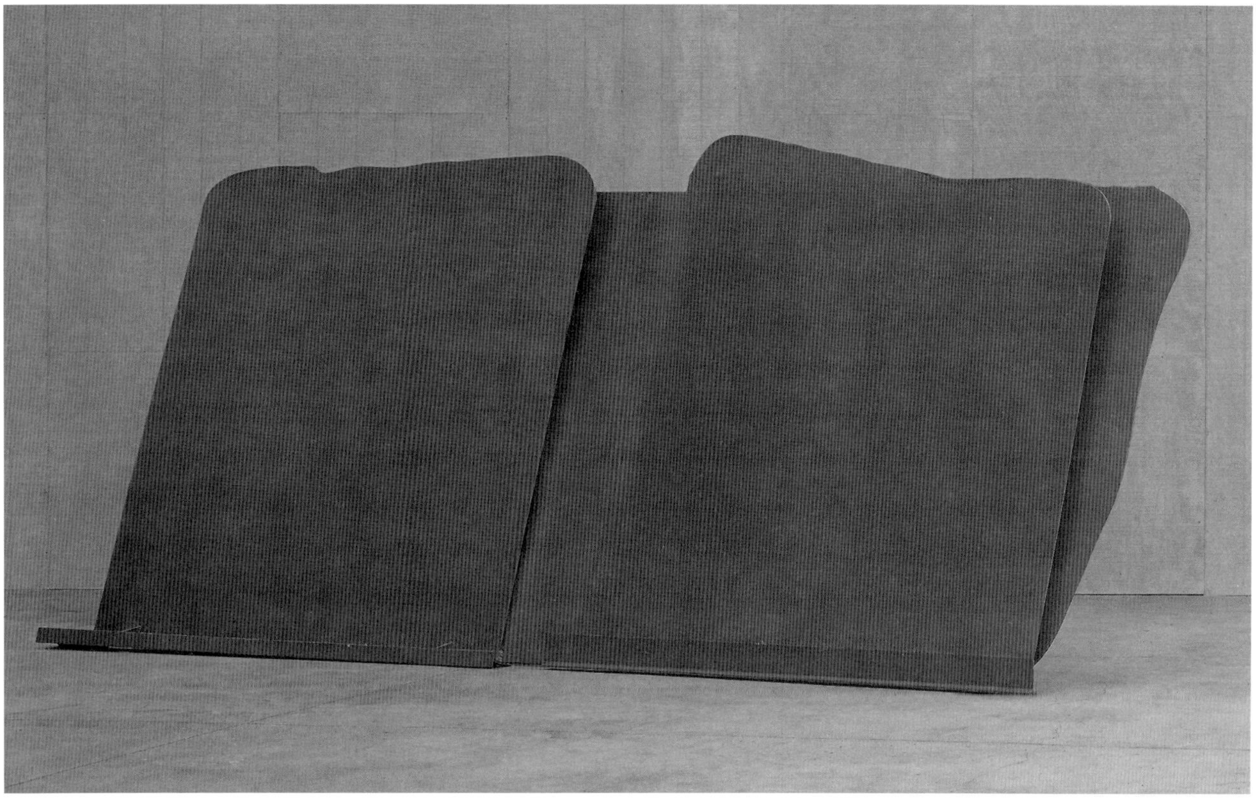

suggest that ultimately Caro's art is more deeply related to the heroic American abstract painting of the 1950s than to the more relaxed, free-floating abstraction of the 1960s with its greater hedonism. Time has shown that Caro's achievement is weightier, his work more truly ambitious, more fully charged with substance, than that of the painters with whom he experienced companionship during the 1960s. Caro's subject matter, as he himself has frequently asserted, is sculpture itself. But if he has eschewed the metaphysics and the ideology which informed the intellectual and aesthetic climate of the great pioneering years of American painting of the 1940s and 1950s, it is in Caro's work, rather than in Smith's, that the painting of these heroic years finds its sculptural counterpart. At a purely visual level the lateral expansion of *Tundra*, punctuated by vertical intervals, and flanked at its extremities by irregular elements, invites analogies with some of the greatest canvases of Barnett Newman and Clyfford Still (fig. 16).

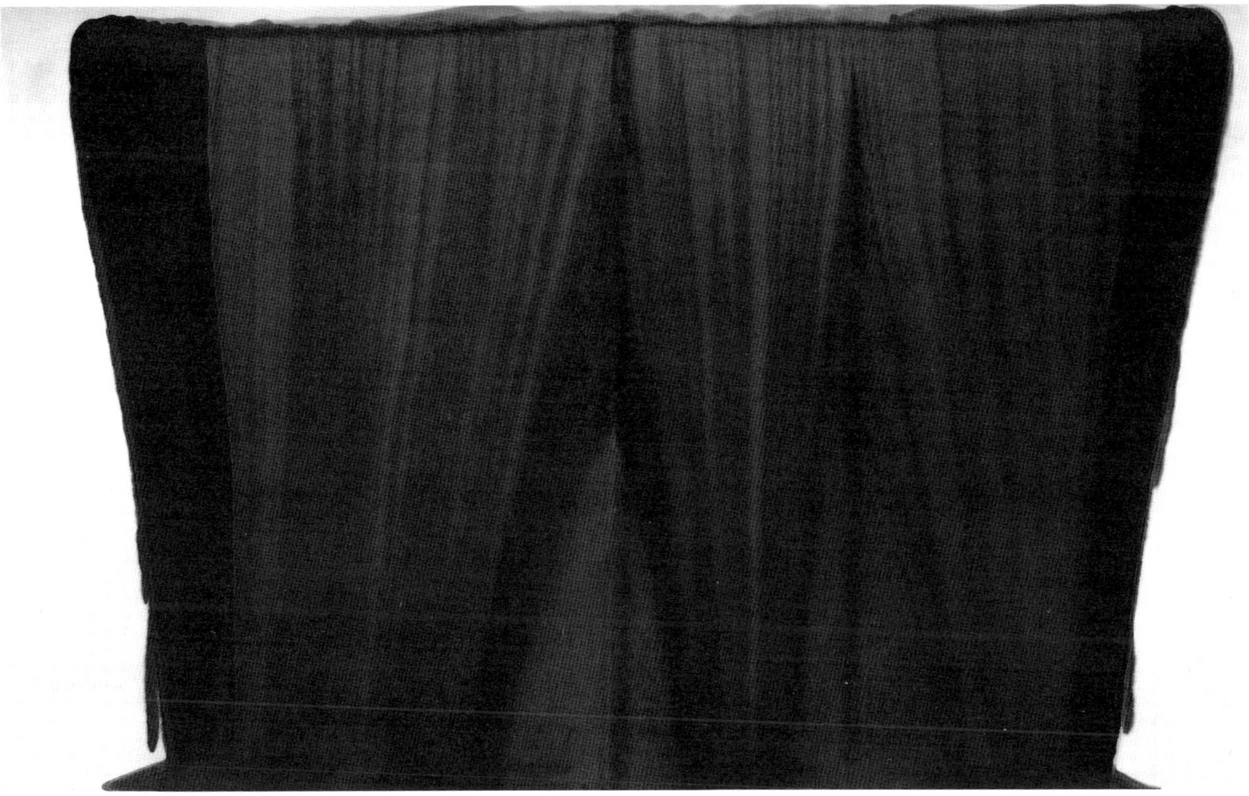

OPPOSITE
13 **ANTHONY CARO**
Double Flats 1974
Steel rusted and varnished
216 x 533.5 x 117 cm
LONDON, ANNELY JUDA FINE ART

ABOVE
14 **MORRIS LOUIS**
Golden Age 1959
Acrylic on canvas
231.1 x 378.5 cm
BELFAST, ULSTER MUSEUM

The *Emma* and the *Catalan* series are both characterised by their use of line. Barcelona, Caro has said, 'is a place all about drawing'[6]; and the quirkiness and fantasy of the city's ubiquitous wrought-iron embellishments inform the *Catalan* series as a whole. The lightness and springiness of the *Emma* sculptures (fig. 17), with their graphic emphasis that defines and controls space rather than simply delineating it, are in part the result of the workshop's relative geographic isolation, which meant that heavy pieces of steel were hard to come by or to transport. But the sculptures also reflect the openness of the Canadian prairies beyond the forest which fringes Emma Lake, and a sculptor's compulsive need to articulate and shape it. Despite the fact that Caro owed so much to American art – and in the eyes of many at the time he had become in a sense an honorary American artist – it is further proof of his stature that, as his art continued to grow and evolve, the painters that begin most often to come

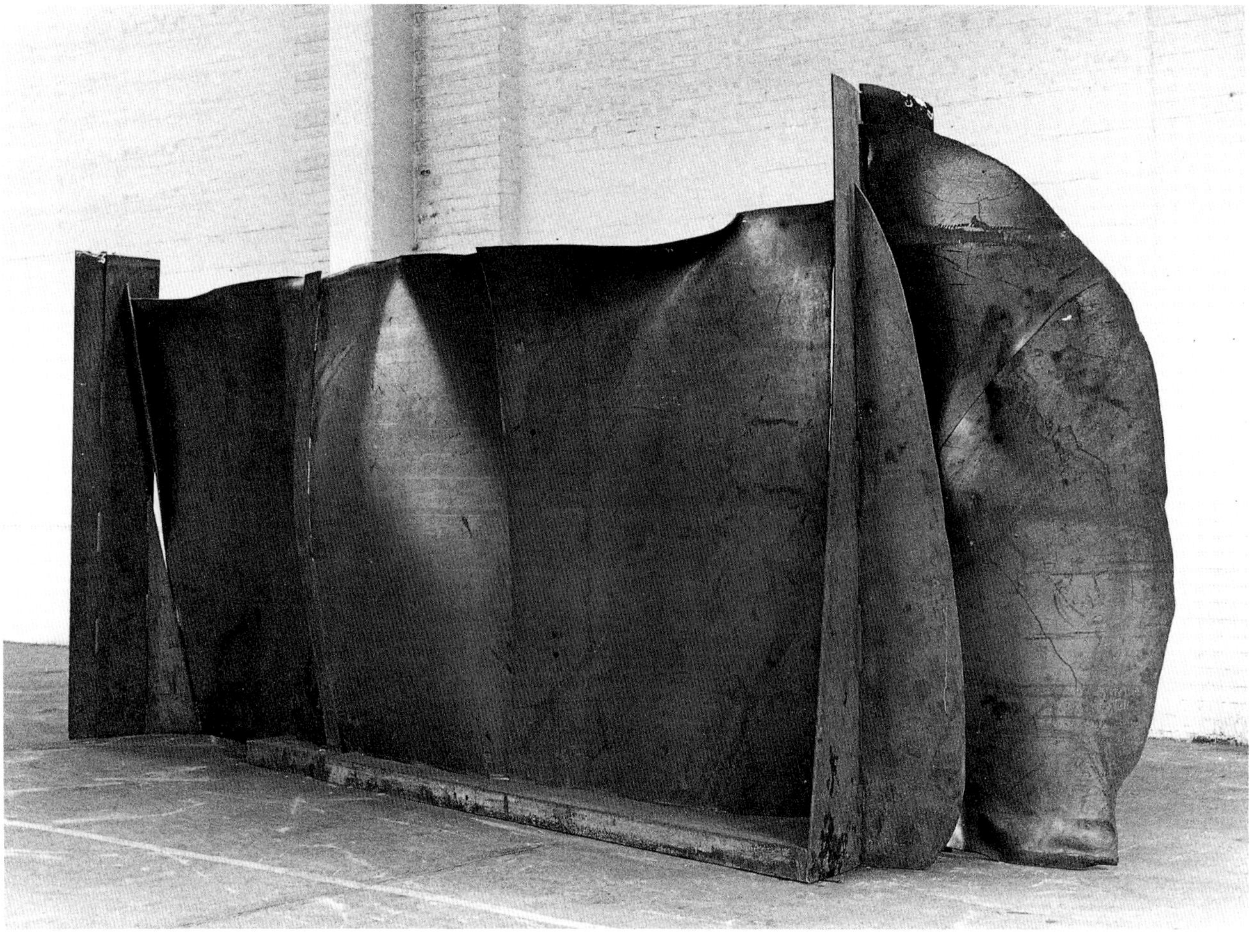

to mind when discussing his work are Matisse and Picasso. The linear configurations of the *Emma* sculptures, for example, recall the welded sculptures Picasso was producing during the 1920s, often with the help of González, but even more vividly those paintings of Picasso's that spelt them out (fig. 18). Yet it might perhaps be fair to say that if ultimately it was Picasso's constructions produced between 1912 and 1914, so intimately related to his *collages*, that were to provide Caro with his sculptural means, Matisse is nevertheless the twentieth-century painter who continues to mean most to him. The influence of Matisse's late *papiers découpés*, themselves in a very real sense surrogate sculptures, is to be felt, for example, in *Orangery* of 1969, and continues to reverberate in his work to this day.

OPPOSITE
15 **ANTHONY CARO**
Tundra 1975
Steel
272 x 579 x 132 cm
LONDON, TATE GALLERY

ABOVE
16 **CLYFFORD STILL**
1956-D 1956
Oil on canvas
290.8 x 406.4 cm
SAN FRANCISCO, MUSEUM OF MODERN ART

It is in what are sometimes called the 'Source Sculptures' that Caro makes most overt reference to painting (although the term is also used to refer to works inspired by other sculpture). These are in one sense tributes to paintings that caught Caro's eye and imagination, that have intrigued and stimulated him. The example of Picasso comes to mind, although Picasso's variations on Velázquez, Delacroix and Manet (amongst many others) show a painter commenting on other painters and on the very nature of painting itself. And when Caro consults past masters, unlike Picasso he does not do so out of a desire to simultaneously communicate with and challenge the art of the past. Picasso's series on *Las Meninas, Les Femmes d'Alger,* and *Le Déjeuner sur l'herbe* are in some ways analogous to musical variations

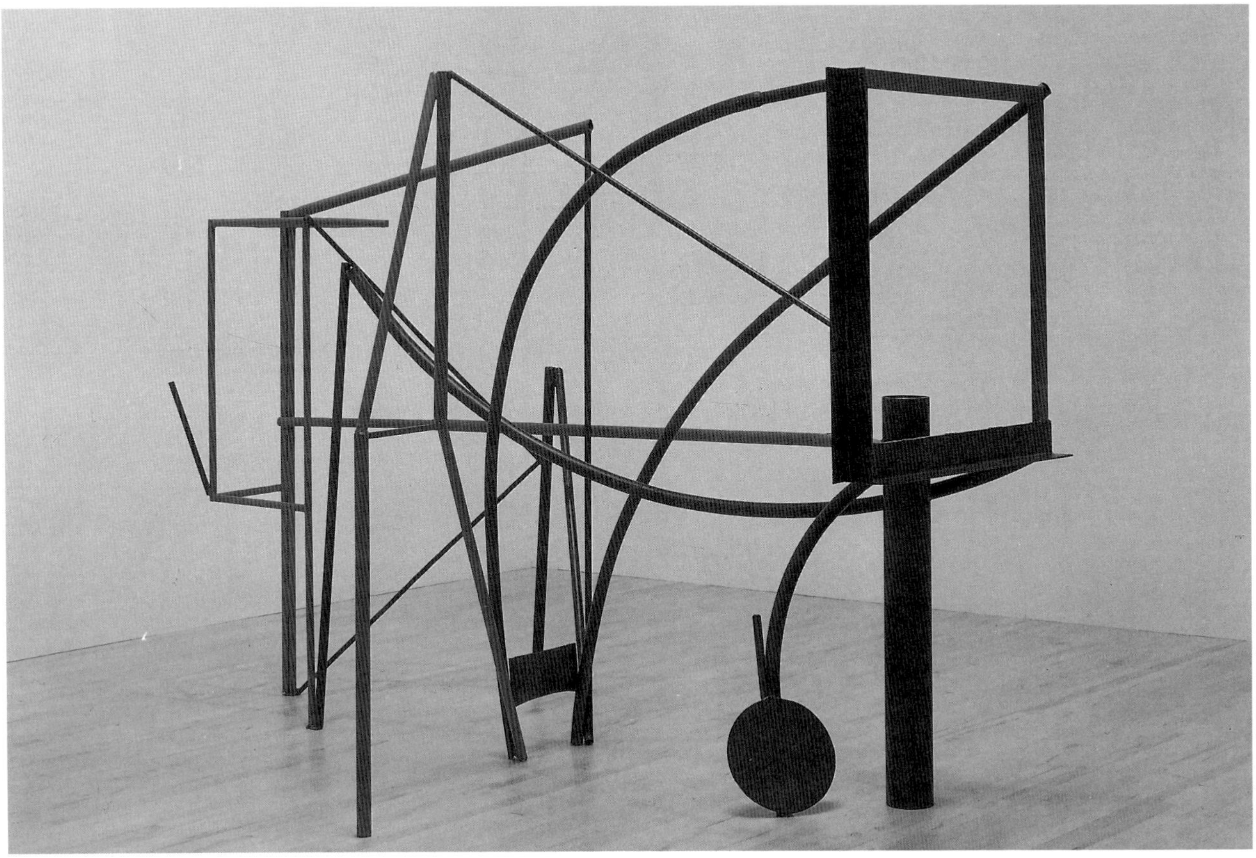

on an acknowledged theme. Caro's sculptural transpositions are of a different order. They, too, acknowledge their sources openly and freely, but there is a feeling of total metamorphosis about them. They have been transformed into something quite else. And just as Caro's experiences of different countries and working environments had encouraged him to change step, to explore new aspects of himself and his talent, so his turning to individual works of art of the past can best be seen as visits to pictorial places, to different turning points in the history of art. These encounters allow him simultaneously to verify his own infinitely varied visual conclusions, to test their emotional and psychological veracity, and so once again to channel himself into extending his sculptural frontiers.

What strikes one most immediately when looking at the paintings and the painters whom Caro has consulted is not so much

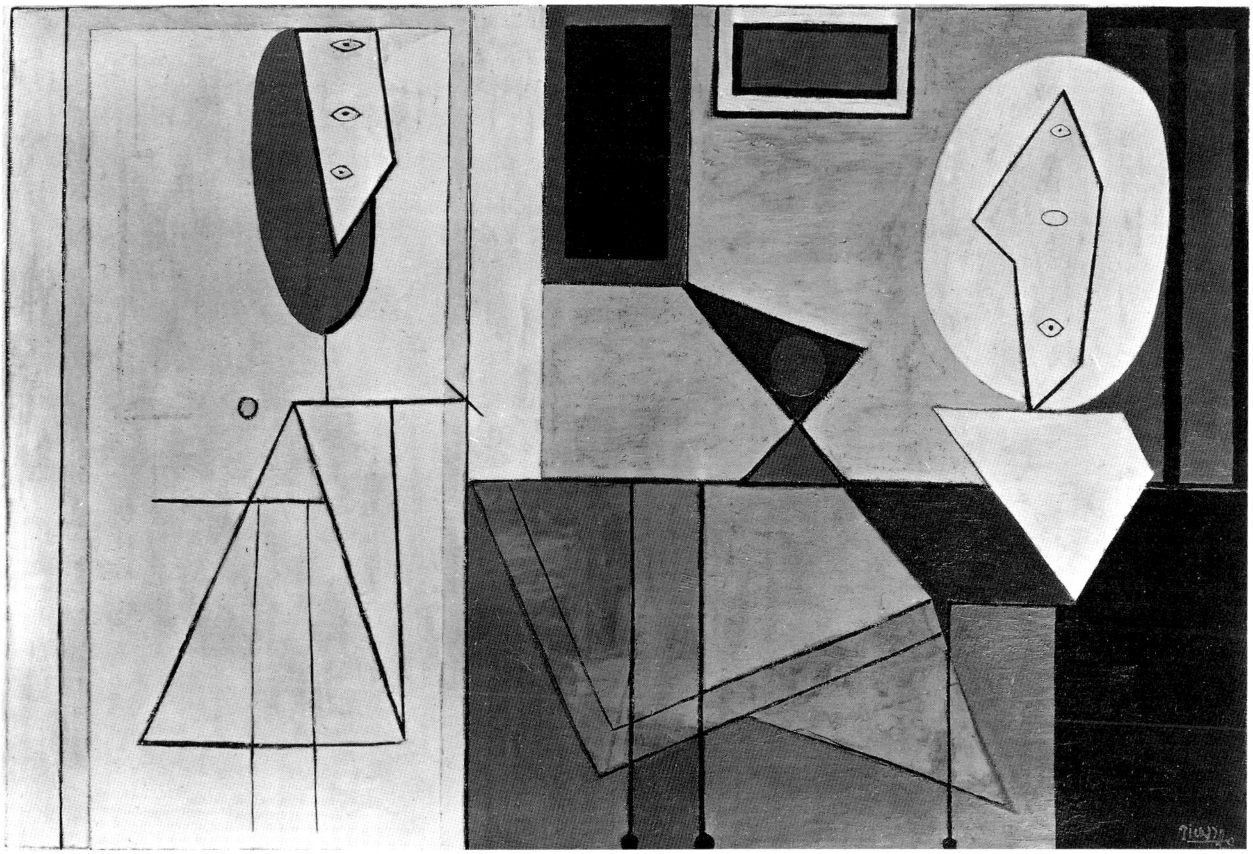

OPPOSITE
17 **ANTHONY CARO**
Emma Dipper 1977
Steel rusted and painted grey
213.5 x 170 x 320 cm
LONDON, TATE GALLERY

ABOVE
18 **PABLO PICASSO**
The Studio 1927–8
Oil on canvas
149.9 x 231.2 cm
NEW YORK, MUSEUM OF MODERN ART

what they have in common, but rather that they are so astonishingly disparate. In 1985 Caro stated: 'Times have changed. Now there is confidence in treating abstraction in sculpture, it's been shown that abstraction can carry emotion. There has been a loosening of the need to make that point. Naturalism versus abstraction isn't the issue; the issue now seems to be how far you can go and still call it art... [although] I continue to believe that the way forward is through a thoroughgoing and deep sort of abstraction.'[7] *Table Piece LXXXVIII, 'The Deluge'* of 1969 (fig.19) has been cited as the first of Caro's works after the masters. But the work received its title only after it had been finished, when William Rubin of the Museum of Modern Art in New York suggested that the frothy, disembodied lightness of the piece reminded him of Leonardo's studies of swirling, eddying water (fig. 20). Caro's first overt references to pictorial mentors were,

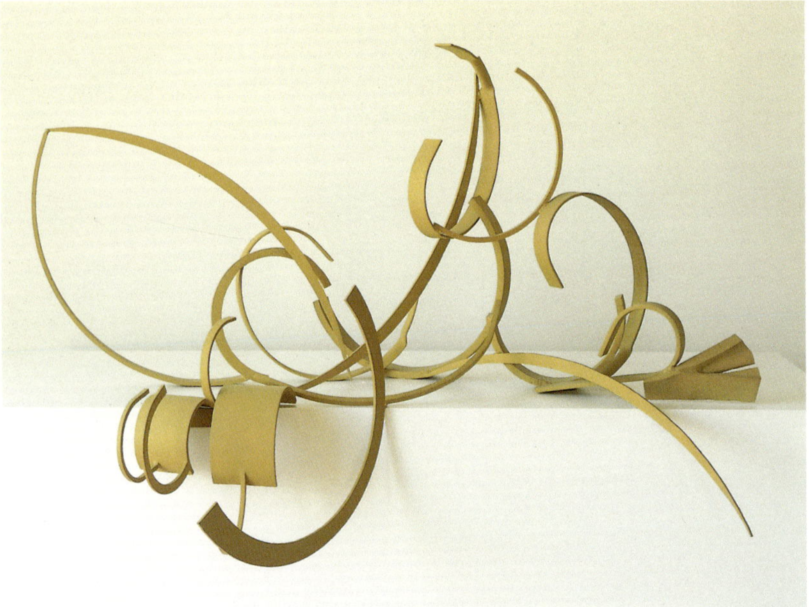

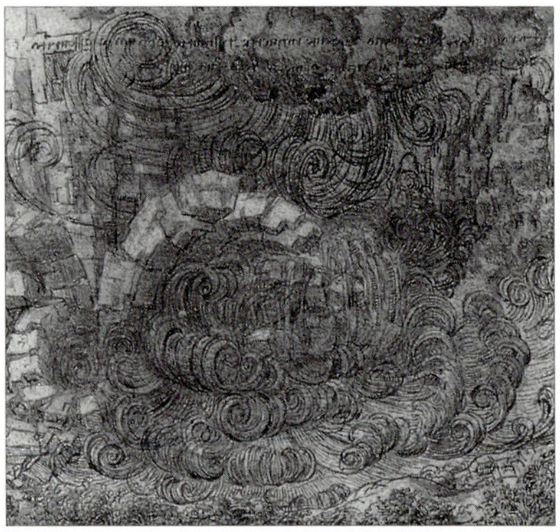

LEFT
19 **ANTHONY CARO**
Table Piece LXXXVIII, 'The Deluge'
1969
Steel painted zinc chromate primer
100.7 x 158.2 x 90.8 cm
NEW YORK, MUSEUM OF MODERN ART

ABOVE
20 **LEONARDO DA VINCI**
Final stage of vision of destruction
(detail) *c.*1517–18
Black chalk and brown and yellow inks on paper
16.2 x 20.3 cm
WINDSOR, ROYAL LIBRARY

OPPOSITE ABOVE LEFT
21 **ANTHONY CARO**
Garland 1970
Steel painted green and red
140 x 429.5 x 376 cm
HARPSWELL, PRIVATE COLLECTION

OPPOSITE ABOVE RIGHT
22 **ANTHONY CARO**
The Moroccans 1984–7
Stoneware, earthenware with stainless steel support
183 x 203 x 172.5 cm
HAKONE-MACHI, THE HAKONE OPEN-AIR MUSEUM

OPPOSITE BELOW
23 **HENRI MATISSE**
The Moroccans 1915–16
Oil on canvas
181.3 x 279.4 cm
NEW YORK, MUSEUM OF MODERN ART

fittingly enough, to Matisse and Picasso. Matisse's *The Moroccans* of 1915–16 (fig. 23) had been the inspiration for *Garland* of 1970 (fig. 21), although here references to the painting are oblique and hard to detect. *The Mosque* of 1979–80 had taken as its starting point the architectural elements at the top left-hand corner of the picture. It is easy to see why Caro responded to this particular work. It is one of the most abstract of all the works Matisse executed between 1914–16, which show him coming to terms with Synthetic Cubist procedures, derived from *collage*. Caro's own *The Moroccans*, of 1984–7 (fig. 22), makes use of approximately the same number of individual elements as *The Mosque*, but it paraphrases Matisse's entire composition and captures its spirit more truly. This sculpture makes use of somewhat surprising materials for a work of this size (stoneware and earthenware above a structural steel support), and this, together with the fact that some of its elements already existed in the workshop and were thus 'found', while others were especially shaped to fulfil a formal function, mirrors the slightly disjunctive quality of the painting. Matisse's masterpiece is an ambiguous work, both spatially and iconographically, and Caro has always responded to works that baffle him.

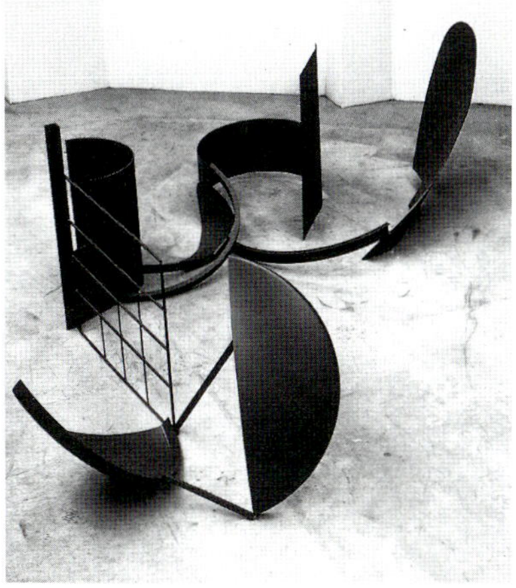

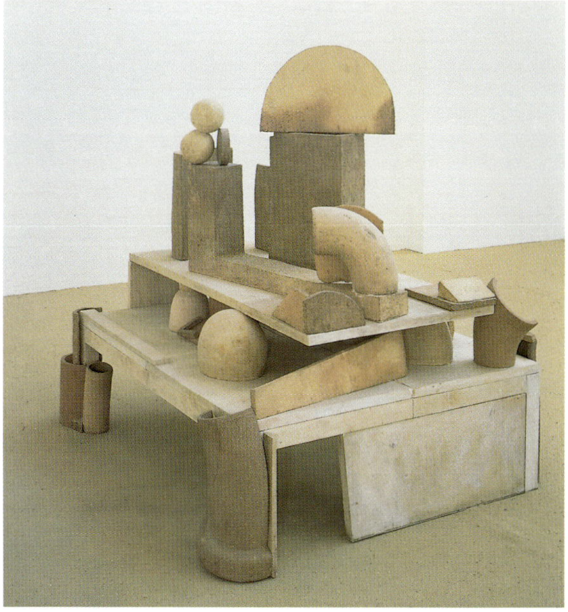

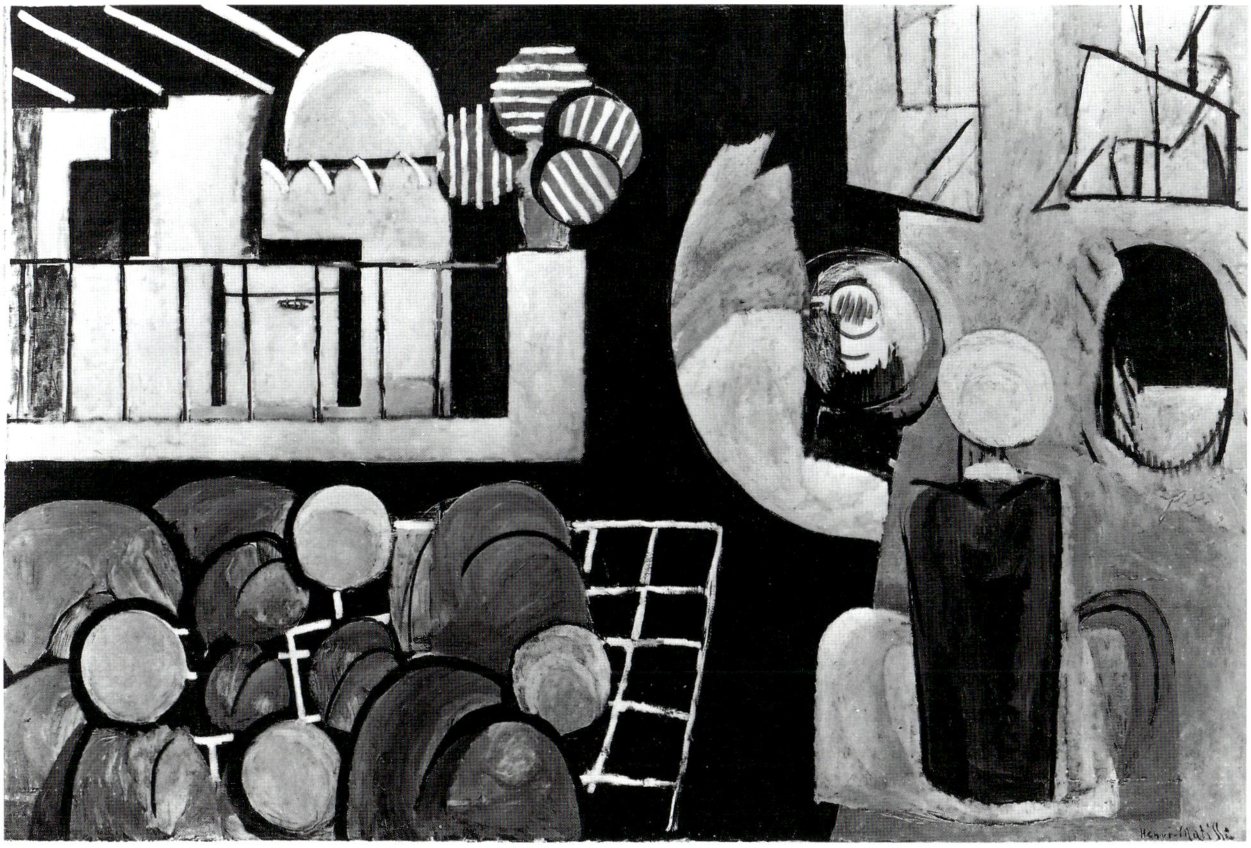

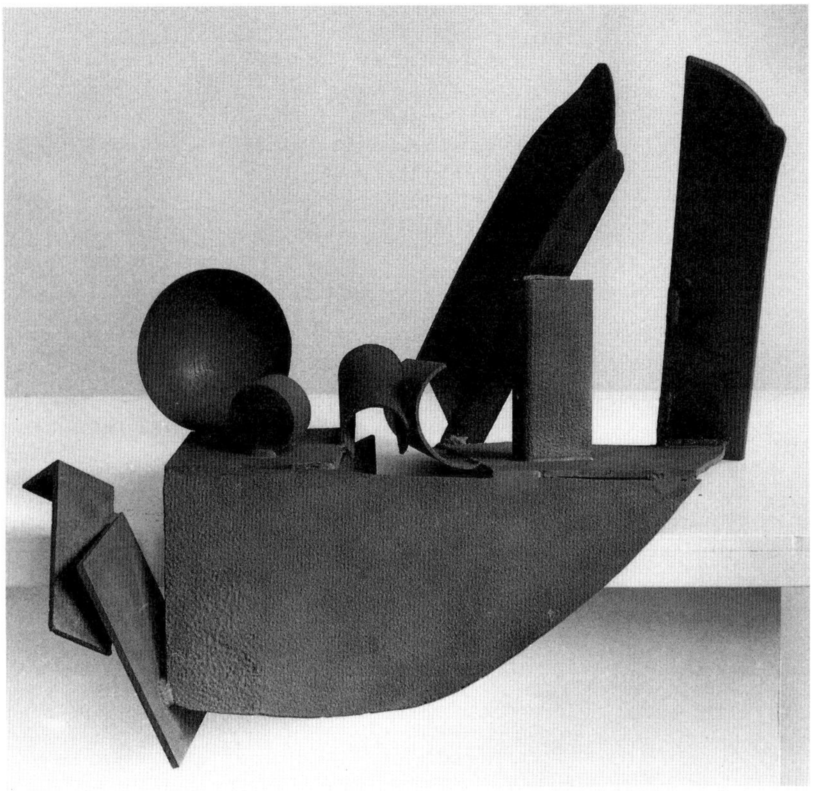

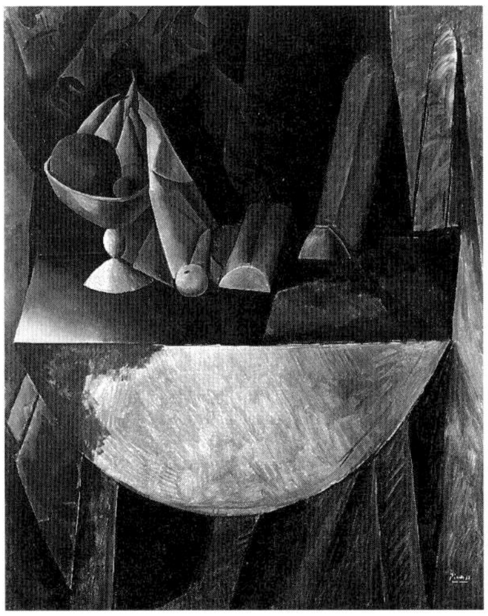

LEFT
24 **ANTHONY CARO**
Table Piece Y-49 (After Picasso) 1985
Steel rusted and waxed
80 x 94 x 78.5 cm
BALTIMORE, COLLECTION OF SHERRY STUART CHRISTHILS III

ABOVE
25 **PABLO PICASSO**
Bread and Fruit Dish on a Table
1908–9
Oil on canvas
164 x 132.5 cm
BASEL, KUNSTMUSEUM

In *Table Piece Y-49 (After Picasso)* of 1985 (fig. 24), Caro turned to an equally pivotal and unusual work, Picasso's *Bread and Fruit Dish on a Table* (1908–9: fig. 25). This began as a composition of five figures, which were subsequently transposed into bread and crockery. Because of this metamorphosis, its appeal to Caro and the lessons it had to teach him speak for themselves. It is also a work that heralds the Cubist revolution, and, like the Caro sculpture derived from it, is in some respects a tribute to Cézanne. The foreground plane of the Picasso, the hanging, curved flap of an extendable table, in Caro's variant drops down below its base or support and thus helps to define his invention of the 'table piece'. Many of the table pieces are amenable to being placed on flat surfaces below eye level. But essentially, like his first floor pieces, they defy the traditional plinth or base, often by spilling over and beyond their supports, dictating and commanding their own independent spatial existences.

In 1985 Caro made a long-delayed trip to Greece which was perhaps to affect him more profoundly than he at first realised. He had always been acutely sensitive to the art of the past, from his student days onwards, and this made him, in certain respects, and like Cézanne and Matisse, a reluctant revolutionary.[8] Caro has often expressed his resistance to moments of high perfection in art. He prefers the beginnings of things, moments of transition, and the exuberance and celebration that follow on from moments of total artistic realisation. In Greece he was most attracted to the immediately pre-classical art of the Temple of Zeus at Olympia (completed about 456 BC). *After Olympia*, 1987, inspired by the sculptures of its two pediments, is possibly the most ambitious of all his sculptures. But it is a problematic work, not least because ideal viewing conditions for it are almost impossible to achieve.[9] *Xanadu*, of 1986–8 (fig. 27), originally also pediment-shaped, is a more cohesive work. In it, significantly enough, are to be found lessons learned by Caro from Matisse's *Bathers by a River* (fig. 26), worked on between 1909 and 1916, and the summation of Matisse's debt to Cubism. It was after the Greek experience that Caro felt free to roam, in his acknowledged sources, from Giotto, so loved by Matisse, right through once again to Matisse himself.

Caro was instinctively drawn to Mantegna's *Triumphs of Caesar* (probably of the 1490s: figs. 29 and 30) because of its patently high ambition. Like the Temple of Zeus at Olympia it heralds a moment of total perfection in art but also stands back from it in anticipation. Its ceremonial and processional qualities reflect those found in so much Greek and Roman art; the debt to Greece is affirmed by Caro's adoption of the pediment shape. And then Mantegna is the steeliest of all Italian Renaissance masters, and steel is the material that is at the core of Caro's art, although from the later 1970s onwards he experimented increasingly with other materials: copper, bronze, clay, wood, even paper. These experiments were in turn to feed back into his use of steel, which has become ever more versatile.

Table Piece Y-92, 'The Triumph of Caesar' (fig. 28) is revealing of Caro's attitude to his sources at many levels. Virtually all the forms that compose it were drawn from his store of existing metal fragments.

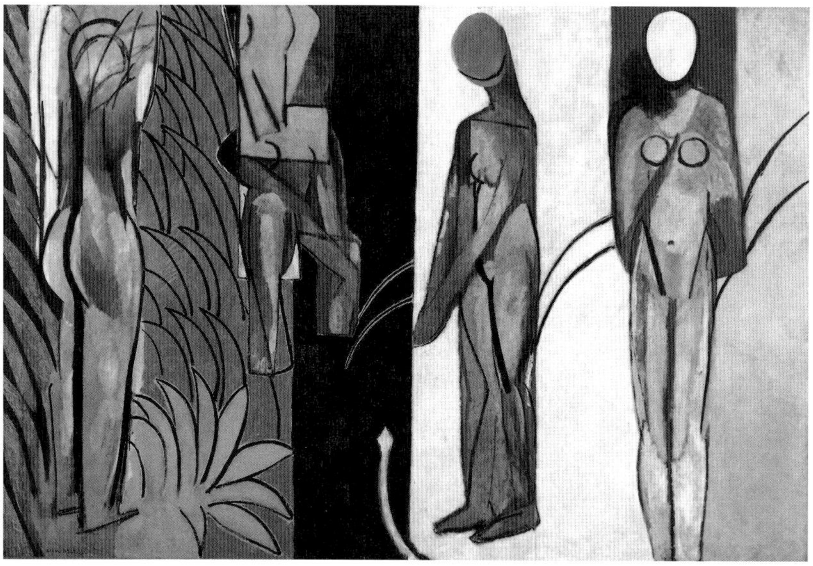

LEFT
26 **HENRI MATISSE**
Bathers by a River
1909, 1913 and 1916
Oil on canvas
259.7 x 389.9 cm
THE ART INSTITUTE OF CHICAGO

OPPOSITE
27 **ANTHONY CARO**
Xanadu 1986–8
Steel waxed
240 x 622 x 160 cm
LONDON, TATE GALLERY
(on loan from Private Collection)

In other words they were not manufactured for the sculpture but rather were selected simply to recall Mantegna's forms at a distance and evoke their spirit. Caro appears to have turned primarily to the third and fourth of Mantegna's great decorations. Interestingly enough, although there is a break between these canvases, a drawing by Mantegna shows that at one point he intended to join them together.[10] But Caro's work is in effect an abstract sculptural procession; it might not be too fanciful to suggest that it is also about the trophies sculpture can win for itself. And he has been stimulated as much if not more by the progression of Mantegna's series as a whole than by specific elements within them. The right angle of the 'table' on which the sculpture stands gives the procession a strong turning or wheeling sensation experienced also in Mantegna's Canvases II and VI (the scenes that link them are viewed more frontally). The ribbon-like, suspended elements at the bottom of the Caro, dropping below the angled ledge of the support, reinforce this feeling but simultaneously pull the composition together, tautening and flattening it.

The same device is exploited in the paraphrase of Manet's *Le Déjeuner sur l'herbe* (fig. 35) but now to give a feeling of cradling, of self-containment to the sculpture (fig. 37). It was, in a sense, inevitable

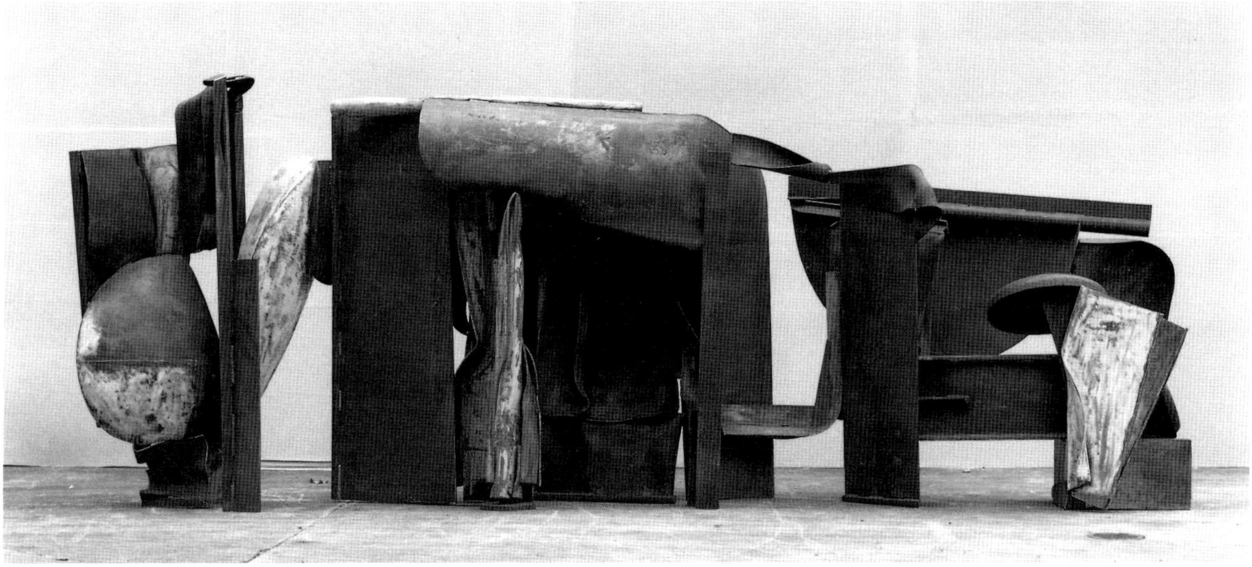

that Caro should turn to this particular work. Perhaps more than any other single work of the nineteenth century it was fundamental to the emergence of the concept of 'Modernism', and subsequently to the definition of it being evolved by Greenberg at the time of his meeting with Caro. 'Realistic, naturalistic art had dissembled the medium, using art to conceal art; Modern art used art to call attention to art', Greenberg declared in 1960.[11] For Greenberg, what characterised modern painting was above all its flatness: 'Modernist painting oriented itself to flatness as it did to nothing else.'[12] To the eyes of many of Manet's contemporaries it was the flatness of *Le Déjeuner sur l'herbe*, with its brilliant frontal lighting, as well as its erotic overtones, that made the picture so shocking. And throughout his life Manet was to be more influential and controversial by virtue of the way he painted, by virtue of the vividness and candour of his technique, than because of what he painted.

As a sculptor Caro was clearly not after flatness, although his work does often aspire to what might be called a three-dimensional, even an architectural, frontality. But then Greenberg had also declared that modern sculpture was about to claim for itself an even greater freedom than that expressed by modern painting. Caro, in his acceptance of this challenge, must have been acutely, if intuitively,

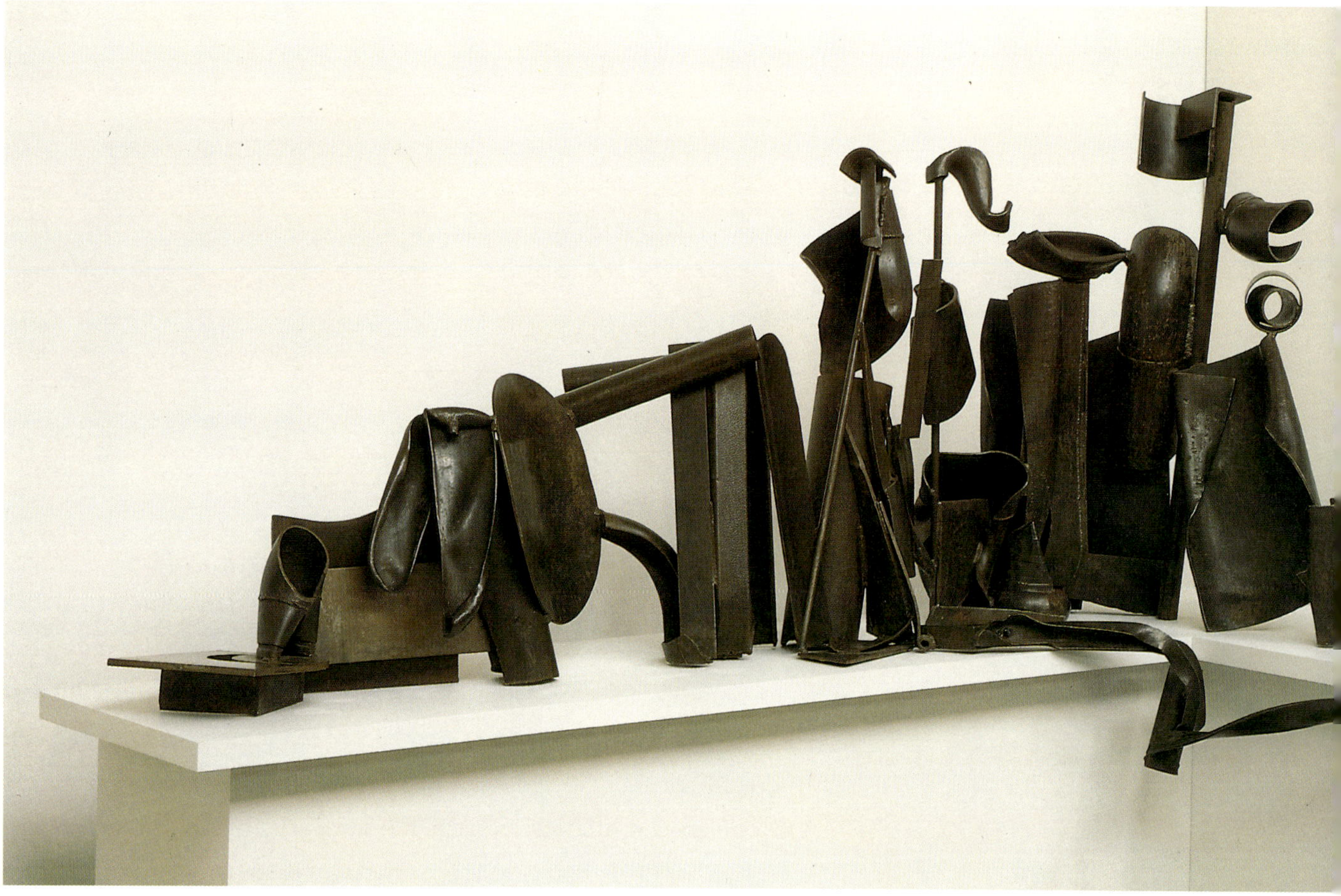

Table Piece Y-92, 'The Triumph of Caesar'

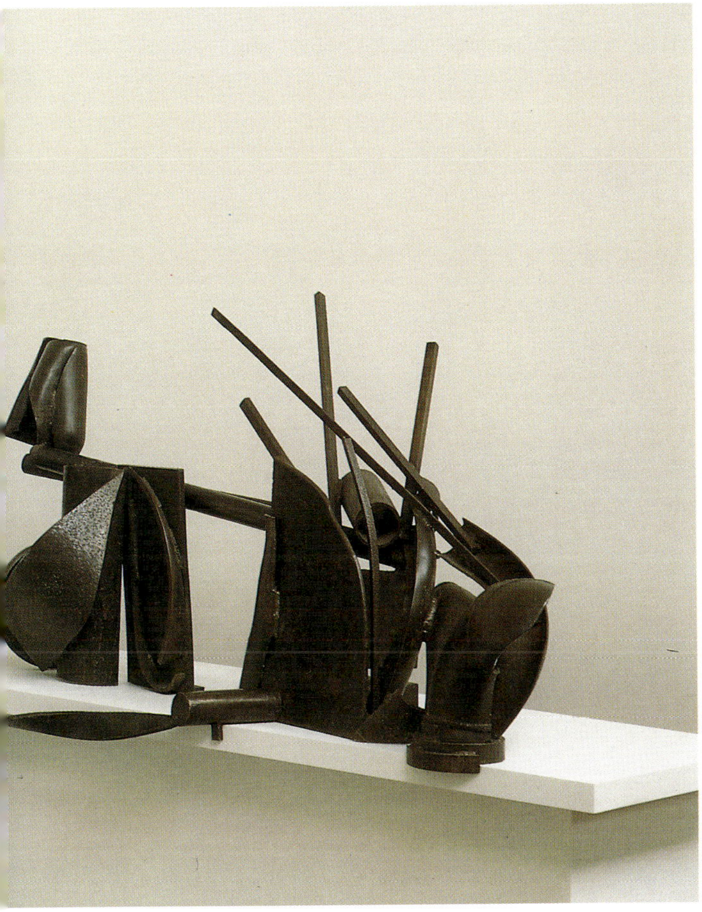

LEFT
28 **ANTHONY CARO**
Table Piece Y-92, 'The Triumph of Caesar'
1987
Steel waxed
157.5 x 343 x 198 cm
HARPSWELL, PRIVATE COLLECTION

BELOW LEFT
29 **ANDREA MANTEGNA**
The Triumphs of Caesar:
Canvas III, 'The Trophy Bearers'
probably 1490s
Tempera on canvas
268 x 278 cm
LONDON, HAMPTON COURT, ROYAL COLLECTION

BELOW RIGHT
30 **ANDREA MANTEGNA**
The Triumphs of Caesar:
Canvas IV, 'The Vase Bearer'
probably 1490s
Tempera on canvas
268 x 279 cm
LONDON, HAMPTON COURT, ROYAL COLLECTION

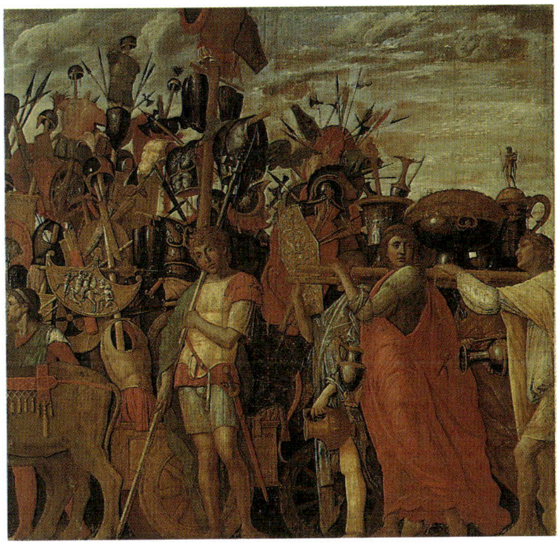

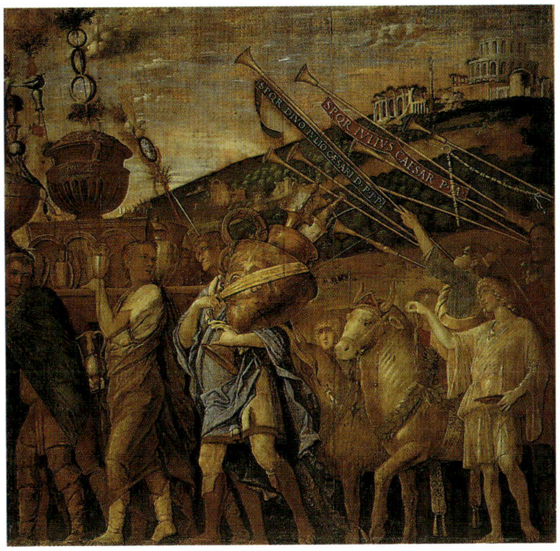

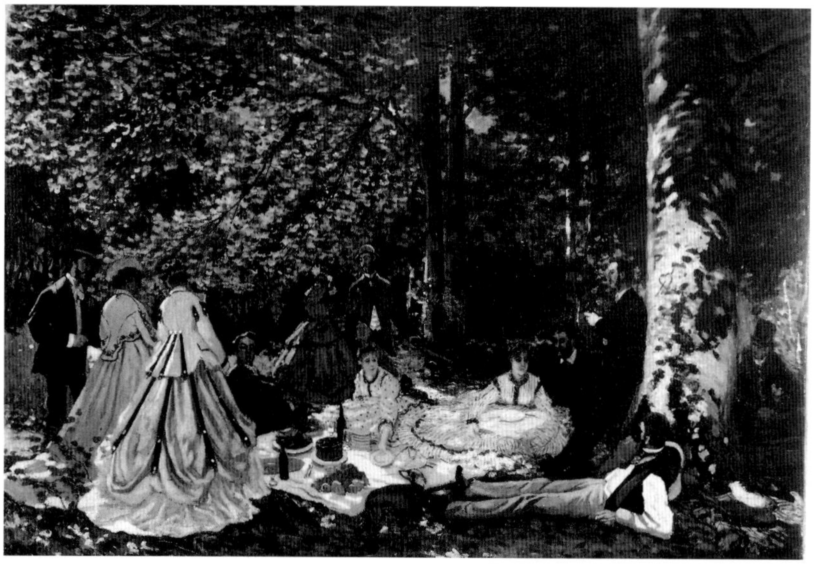

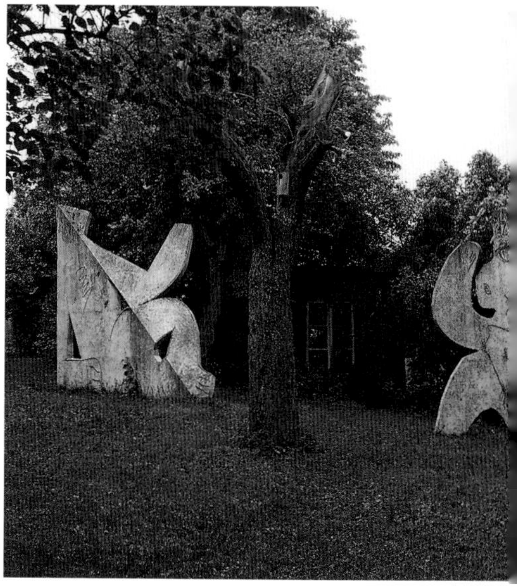

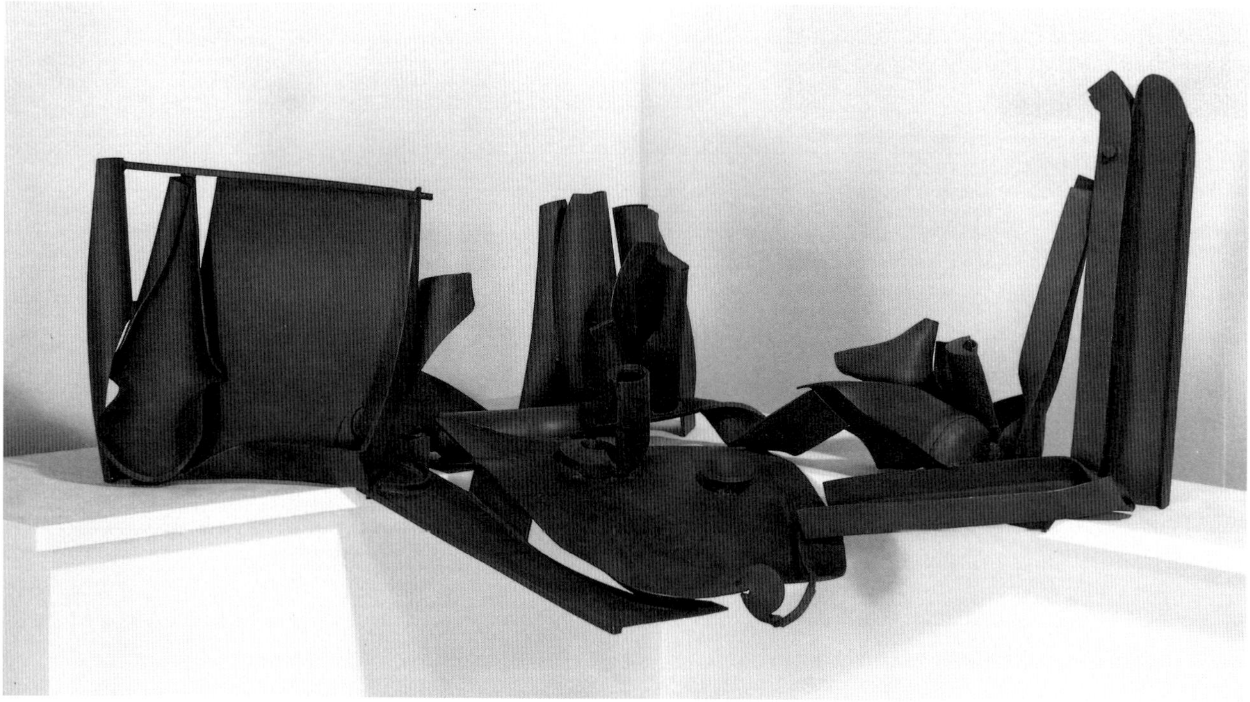

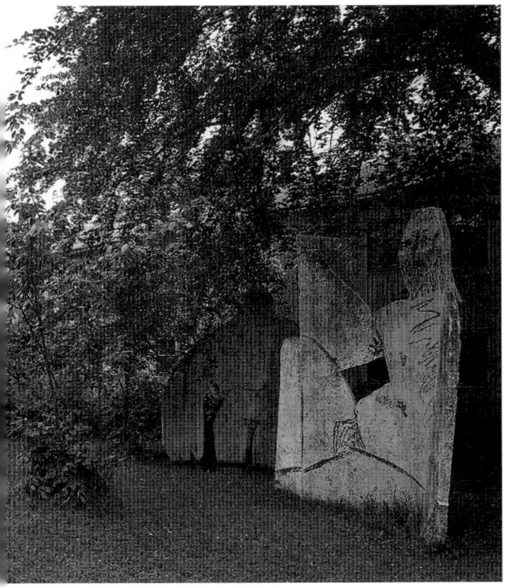

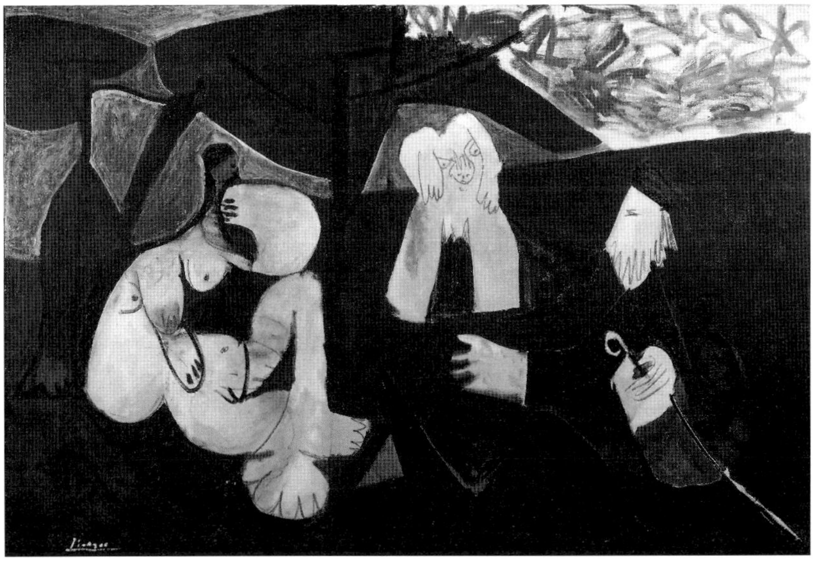

OPPOSITE ABOVE
31 **CLAUDE MONET**
Le Déjeuner sur l'herbe 1866
Oil on canvas
130 x 181 cm
MOSCOW, STATE PUSHKIN MUSEUM OF FINE ARTS

ABOVE CENTRE
32 **PABLO PICASSO** with **CARL NESJAR**
Le Déjeuner sur l'herbe 1965–6
Sandblasted concrete
Height 3 to 5 metres
STOCKHOLM, MODERNA MUSEET

ABOVE RIGHT
33 **PABLO PICASSO**
Le Déjeuner sur l'herbe, after Manet 1960
Oil on canvas
130 x 195 cm
GILBERT DE BOTTON FAMILY FOUNDATION

OPPOSITE BELOW
34 **ANTHONY CARO**
Table Piece Y-97, 'Déjeuner sur l'herbe I' 1989
Steel, rusted and waxed
129.5 x 259 x 172.5 cm
HAMILTON, ONTARIO, MCMASTER MUSEUM OF ART

aware of his relationship to the Modernist tradition and how he was helping to shape it. What makes Manet such a compelling exemplar for Caro is that Manet had felt the need to test the validity of his vision in the face of the art of the past. Manet's earliest surviving paintings are copies after the masters, and in *Le Déjeuner sur l'herbe* he makes reference both to Titian and, indirectly, to Raphael (fig. 36). All these factors were what had already attracted Picasso to the picture, when, between 1959 and 1962, he executed over a hundred variations on it (fig. 33), finally transposing it into folded cardboard 'maquettes' for sculptures. Four of these were used to produce, in sandblasted concrete, the gigantic sculptural complex installed in the gardens of Stockholm's Moderna Museet in 1966 (fig. 32).[13]

Early in 1989 Caro had somewhat surprisingly executed a first '*Déjeuner sur l'herbe*' (fig. 34), after Monet – surprisingly because Impressionism was so little amenable to sculpture as a medium. Caro's reinvention of the Monet has about it a relaxed, pastoral air, reinforced by a strong feeling of horizontality. A comparison with the painting (fig. 31) demonstrates Caro's ability to synthesise and to simplify. '*Déjeuner sur l'herbe II*' (fig. 37) is a more ambitious undertaking and the pictorial and psychological tensions inherent in

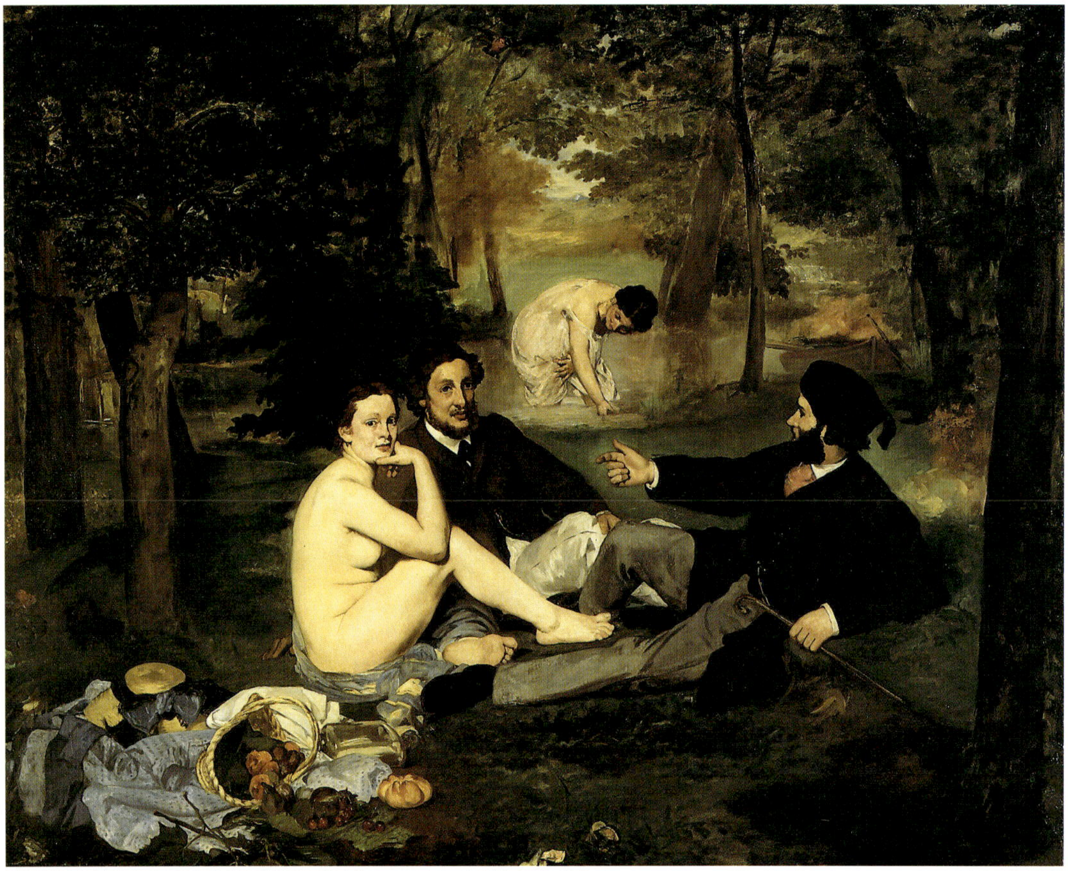

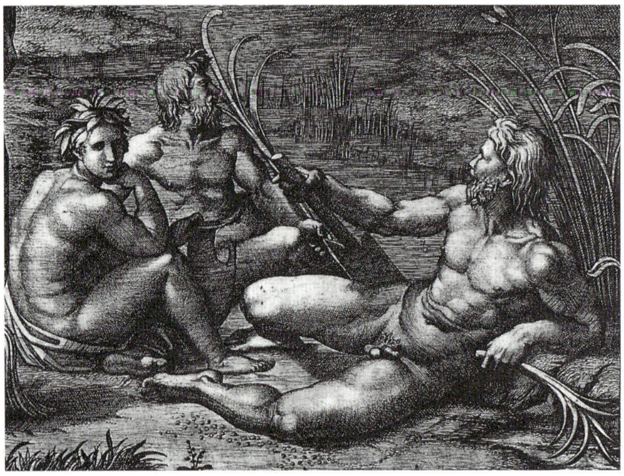

ABOVE
35 **EDOUARD MANET**
Le Déjeuner sur l'herbe
1863
Oil on canvas
208 x 264 cm
PARIS, MUSÉE D'ORSAY

LEFT
36 **MARCANTONIO RAIMONDI**
The Judgement of Paris (detail)
1525–30
Engraving after lost drawings by Raphael
29.8 x 44.2 cm
LONDON, THE BRITISH MUSEUM

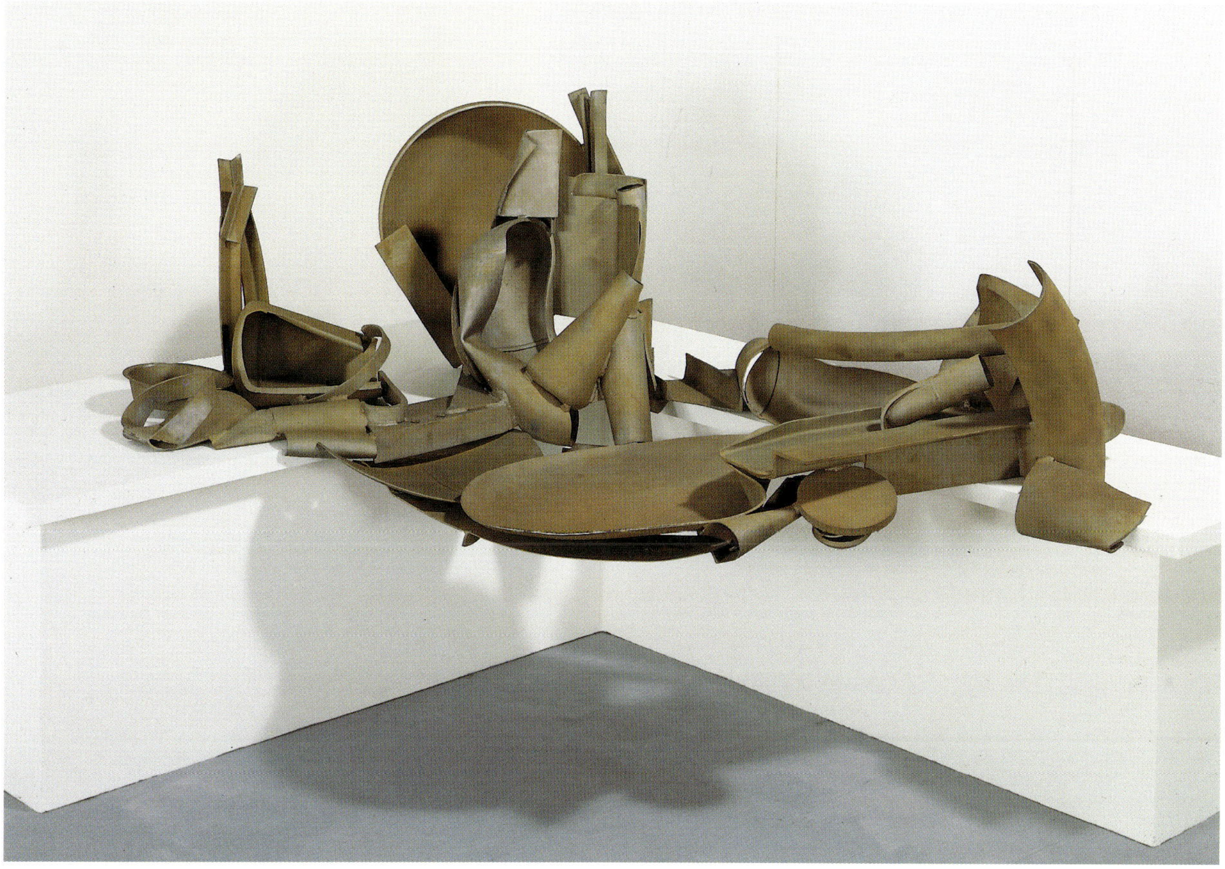

37 **ANTHONY CARO**
Table Piece Y-98, 'Déjeuner sur l'herbe II'
1989
Steel rusted and fixed
82 x 280 x 185.5 cm
LONDON, PRIVATE COLLECTION

Manet's masterpiece are orchestrated into a baroque fantasy that resolves conflict and disjunction into a visual symphony. The main configurations of the Manet – the still life, the naked model and her partner, the second, bathing woman and the trees behind her, the reclining male figure to the right – have all found their abstract visual counterparts. It is worth remarking that Manet's subliminally shaded outlines, which by some pictorial alchemy succeed in giving his flattened forms a subsidiary sense of bulk and weight, find a parallel in the way in which the narrow, compressed side views of Caro's sculptures help to inform one of their density. Here the side views dissolve into liquid ripples. The soft, golden patina, in contrast to the dark, metallic sheen of the *'Triumph'*, reminds one of Manet's avowed intent to create effects that were 'blonder' than nature. Caro once remarked: 'What I like is sensuousness and crispness together.'[14] No painter could better combine these qualities than Manet.

During the 1980s as Caro's work gained in richness and complexity, it increasingly acknowledged affinities with Baroque art, in marked contradistinction to the angularity and spareness of the 1960s. In 1987 he turned to Rubens's great *Descent from the Cross* (fig. 39) from Antwerp Cathedral, of about 1612. It was the visual generosity of Rubens's art, the cornucopia-like aspect of his talent to which Caro responded, just as at the opposite end of the spectrum he may have been unconsciously attracted to the irascibility and spikiness of temperament that informed Mantegna's art.[15] The transcription from Rubens (fig. 38) is the one in which Caro stands emotionally furthest away from his source. His other variants have about them an intuitive psychological rightness, a sense of identification with the painting being studied and with each painter's attitude to his subject. But in Caro's art, as in that of Matisse, there is little room for grief or pain, although a note of tragedy informs the sculptures after Rembrandt, Goya and Van Gogh. This might make his choice of the Crucifixion as a theme seem strange, yet this sculpture had as its starting point a simple formalistic premise. After his return from Greece Caro had become intrigued by the pediment form and how it conditioned the sculpture contained within it. Now he felt the urge to seek

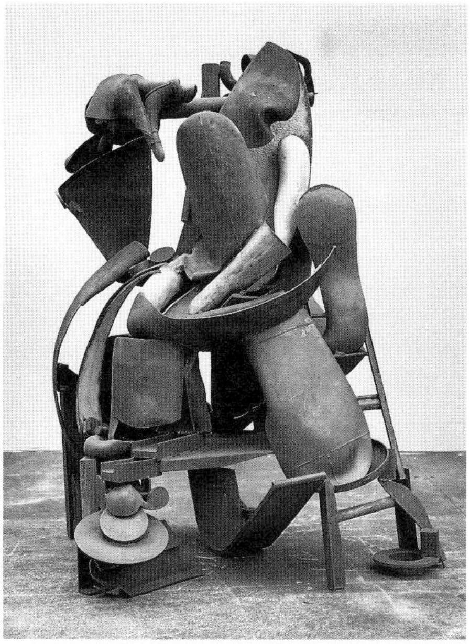

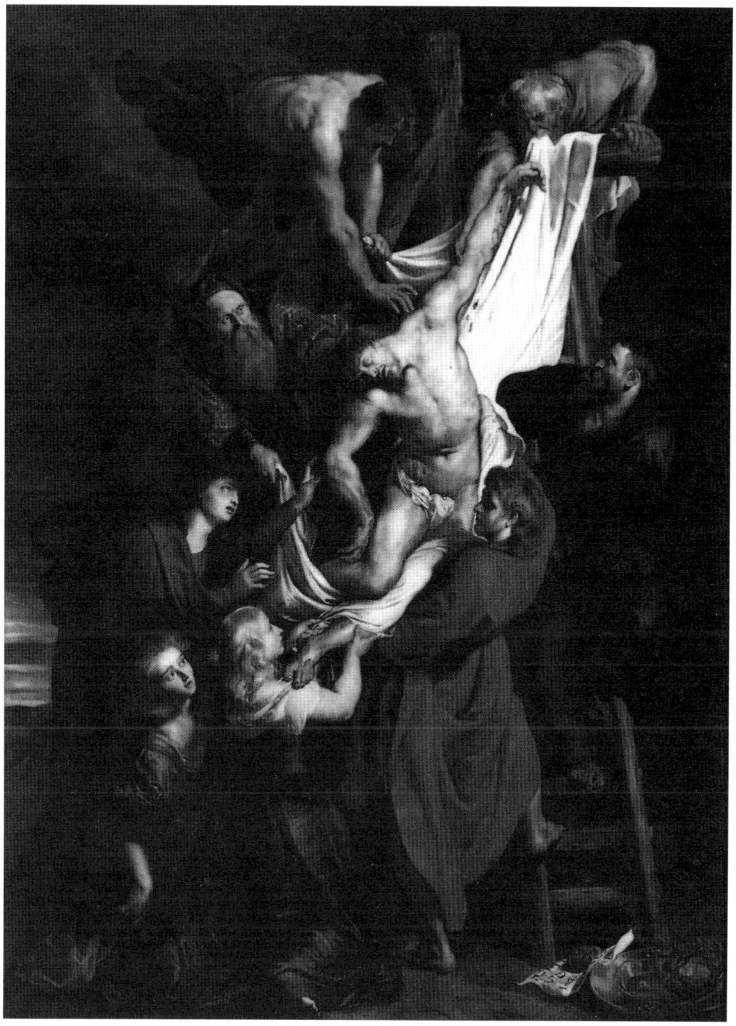

ABOVE
38 **ANTHONY CARO**
Descent from the Cross (After Rubens)
1987–8
Steel rusted and waxed
244 x 185.5 x 160 cm
FORT WORTH, TEXAS, MODERN ART MUSEUM

RIGHT
39 **PETER PAUL RUBENS**
Descent from the Cross c.1612
Oil on panel
420 x 310 cm
ANTWERP CATHEDRAL

for an internal sculptural element which would structure the elements around it – the cross was the most obvious and elementary. In 1967 Caro had stated: 'Part of the problem of sculpture today is the problem of axis: to make it freer, to get rid of a vertical and horizontal axis, and to see if one could make a structure which had no central core at all – where the only axis that spectators were left with would be their own eyes, and their own up and down.'[16] But it is characteristic of Caro, and a particular source of strength to him as the sort of artist he is, that he has periodically been prepared to stop, to take stock and if necessary even to contradict himself in order to give fresh impetus to his work.

Descent from the Cross (After Rembrandt)

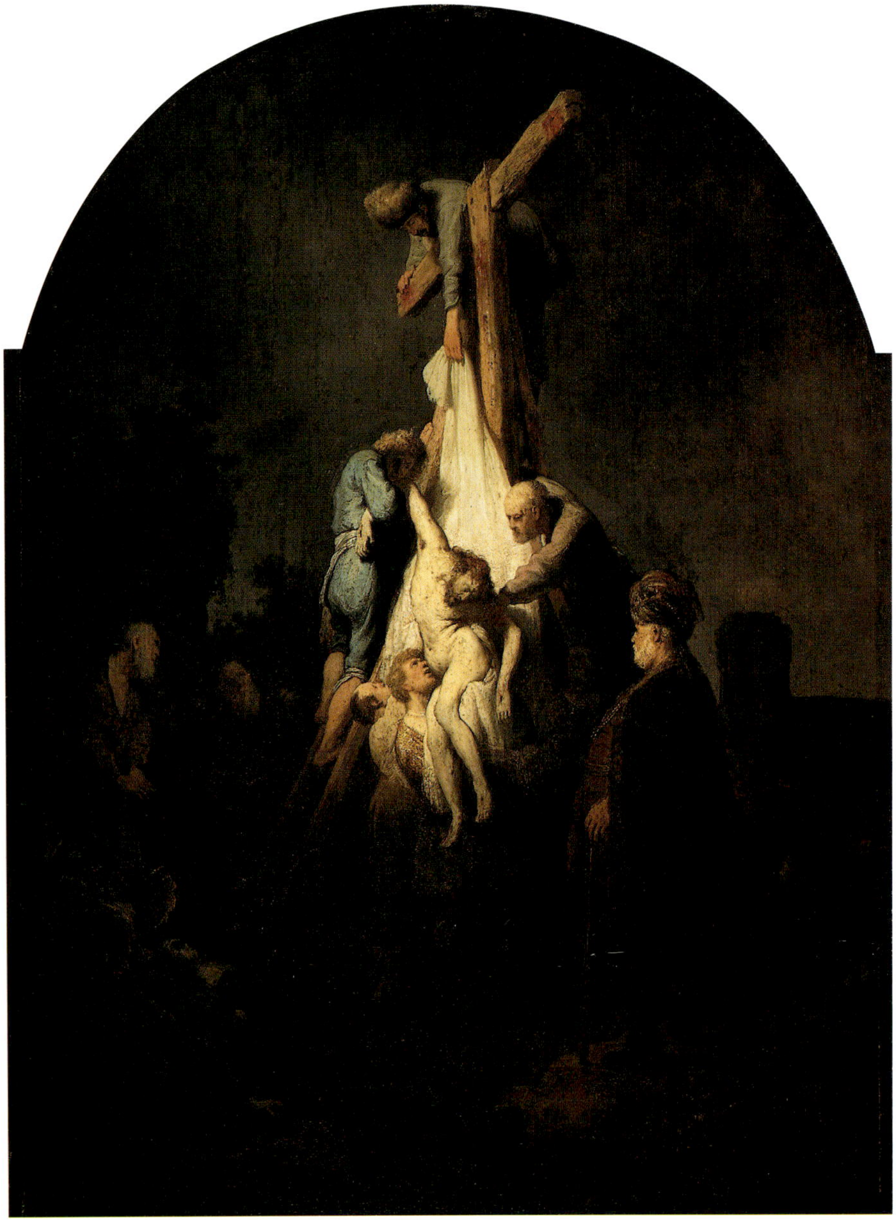

40 **REMBRANDT**
Descent from the Cross
*c.*1633
Oil on panel
89.4 x 65.2 cm
MUNICH, ALTE PINAKOTHEK

41 **ANTHONY CARO**
Descent from the Cross
(After Rembrandt) 1989–90
Brass and bronze cast and welded
221 x 120 x 112 cm
CONSEIL GÉNÉRAL DU VAL-DE-MARNE

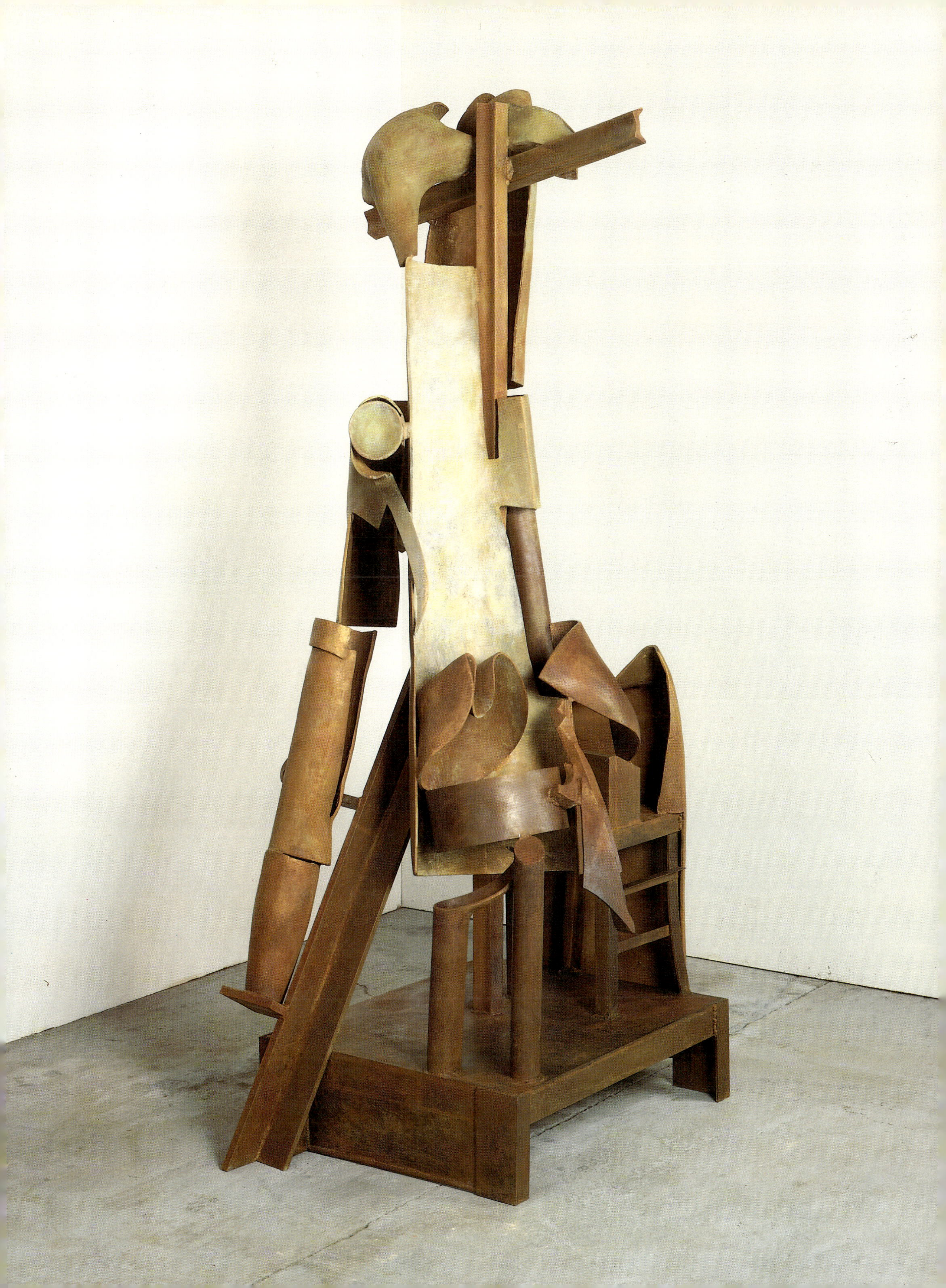

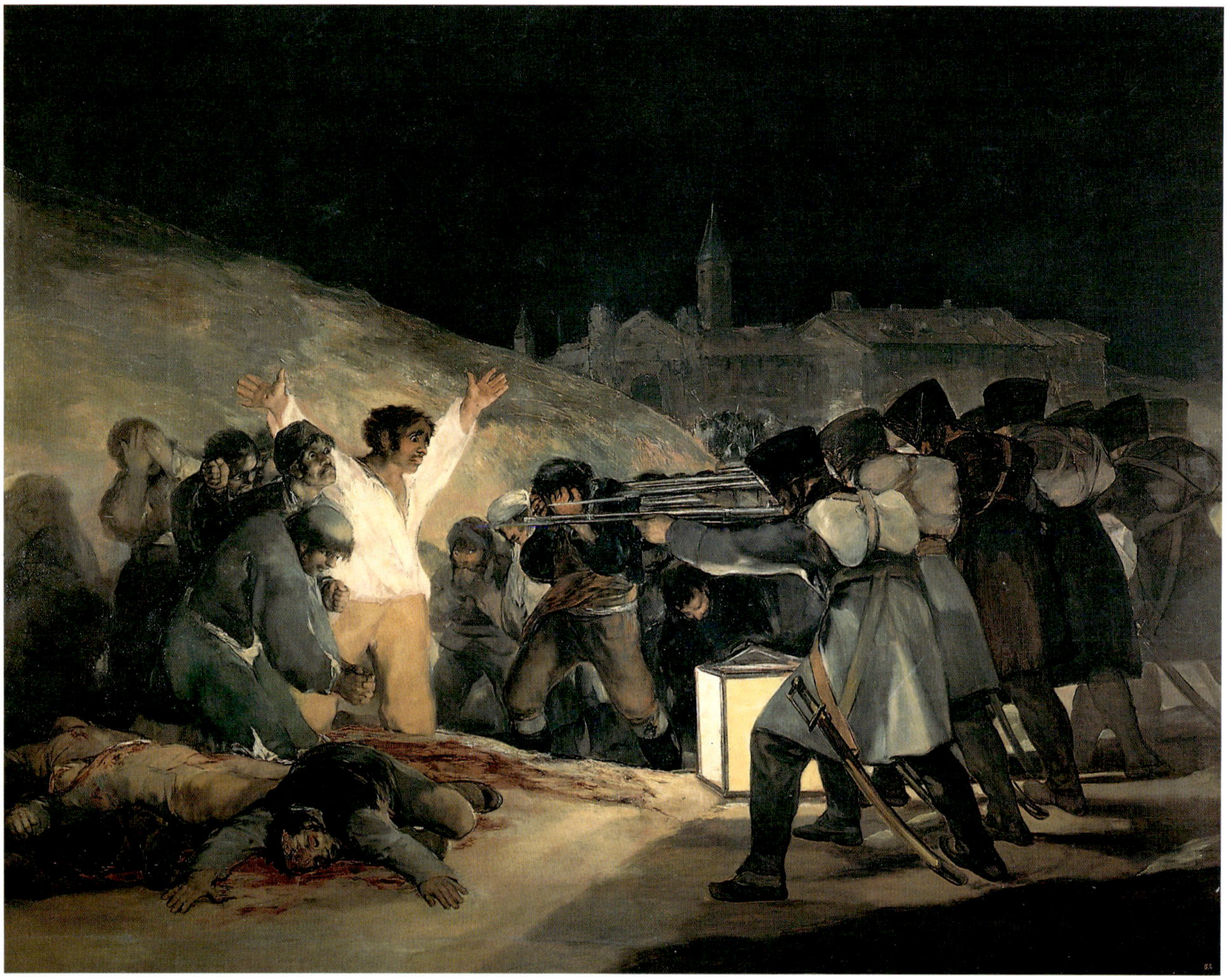

42 **FRANCISCO GOYA**
The Third of May, 1808, at Madrid
1814
Oil on canvas
266 x 345 cm
MADRID, MUSEO DEL PRADO

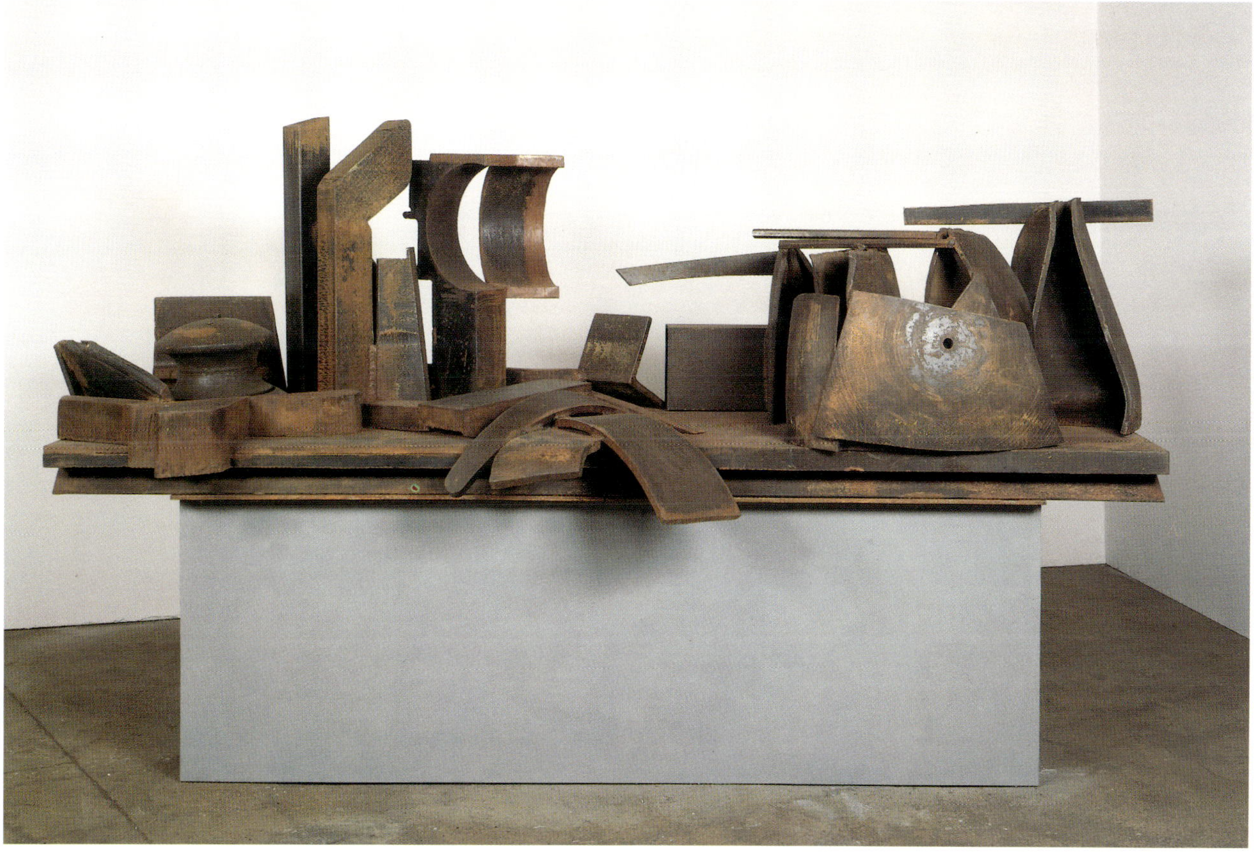

43 **ANTHONY CARO**
Act of War (After Goya)
1994–5
Steel rusted and waxed on steel base (painted grey)
98 x 286 x 130 cm
LONDON, ANNELY JUDA FINE ART

From Rubens, Caro moved on to Rembrandt, and there are two transcriptions from Rembrandt's own *Descent from the Cross* (fig. 40), which was executed some two decades after the Rubens. While Rubens's canvas is vast, the Rembrandt is small in scale, but it is informed by the same monumentality and by an even greater expressive force. Rembrandt must surely have known of the engraving made from the Rubens by Lucas Vorsterman in which the composition is, naturally, reversed. The simpler of Caro's two variations (fig. 41) is the more successful and has about it a genuine poignancy. It reduces and abstracts from its source, as Rembrandt had done from Rubens. Although forms corresponding to the body of Christ can still be identified, it is the whole downward movement of the composition, the feeling of death or emptiness, sliding into the huddled, receiving aggregation of shapes below that tells its story. As a single example of the way that just a few abstract elements can be charged with emotive power, the forms that replace the male figure to the upper left of the shroud, and which in the Rembrandt control the descent of Christ's body, have here become somehow helpless, movingly inadequate to their task.

But the most emotive sculptures after the masters are those that refer to Goya and Van Gogh. *Act of War*, 1994–5 (fig. 43), after Goya's *The Third of May, 1808, at Madrid*, of 1814 (fig. 42), is unique in two respects. It was inspired by the events in Bosnia and by the images of violence and suffering that appeared almost instantaneously in the public press and on television screens all over the world. Manet had consulted the same Goya to express the outrage he shared with other French liberals over the execution of the Emperor Maximilian in Mexico in 1867 (fig. 44). This is the only work by Caro, by temperament an apolitical artist, which comments on a contemporary world event. Although the forms it employs are abstractions, among Caro's works after old master paintings, it is the sculpture that corresponds most faithfully to its source. It is also the most frontal and confrontational. One of the factors which lends the Goya its power is the way in which the French executioners with their heavy headgear seem so anonymous while their Spanish victims are in ordinary clothes

44 **EDOUARD MANET**
The Execution of Maximilian
about 1867–8
Oil on canvas (four fragments laid down on a single support)
193 x 284 cm
LONDON, NATIONAL GALLERY

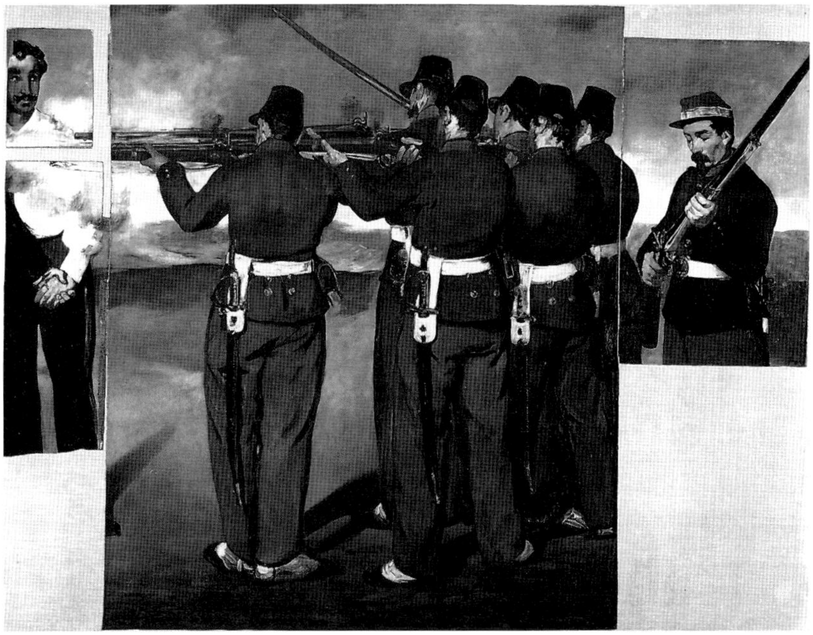

or in a state of undress, totally vulnerable. In Caro's version the abstract forms of the executioners are topped not by elements which might read as substitutes for heads and hats, but by the rifle forms themselves. The pivotal shape to the left which receives their discharge, arches simultaneously backwards in recoil and forwards in acceptance of the violence which has been inflicted upon it.

The five variants on *Van Gogh's Chair* of 1888 (fig. 45) are the only sculptures after the masters to form a true series, and they were executed after the National Gallery had asked if Caro would produce something related to a work in its own Collection. Quite recently Caro stated: 'In the 1960s there were forbidden areas. Sculpture is made of the same stuff artifacts are made of. It can so easily become inexpressive, another artifact. In the 1960s we did everything to avoid allowing our work to look like an insect or a piece of furniture. Nowadays abstraction is so firmly established within the language of sculpture that it no longer requires that sort of defence.'[17] Caro was attracted to the Van Gogh because of its earthiness, its simplicity, what he calls its 'objecthood', because it depicted an object of everyday use, in this case heavily layered in meanings. Characteristically, Caro has conflated

Chairs (After Van Gogh)

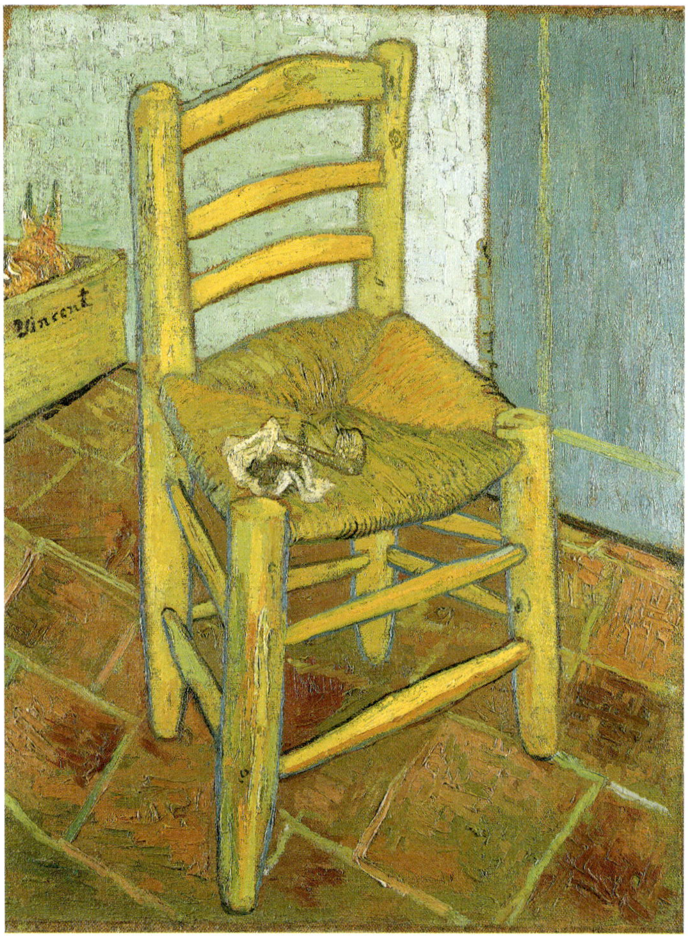

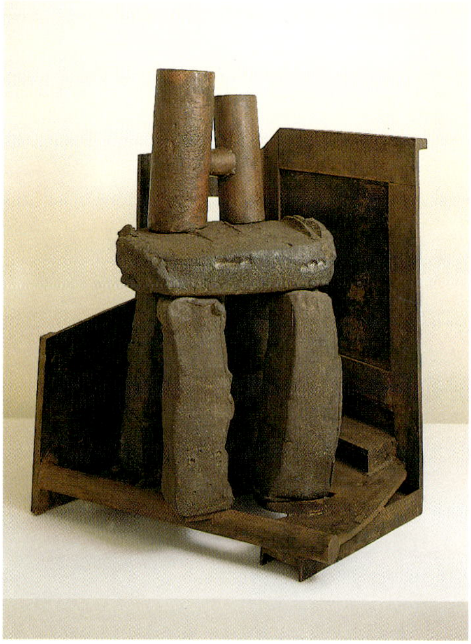

45 **VINCENT VAN GOGH**
Van Gogh's Chair 1888
Oil on canvas
91.8 x 73 cm
LONDON, NATIONAL GALLERY

ABOVE RIGHT
46 **ANTHONY CARO**
Chair V (After Van Gogh) 1997
Stoneware and rusted steel waxed
93 x 71 x 65 cm
LONDON, ANNELY JUDA FINE ART

BELOW RIGHT
47 **ANTHONY CARO**
Chair III (After Van Gogh) 1997
Stoneware and rusted steel waxed
86.5 x 58.5 x 81.5 cm
LONDON, ANNELY JUDA FINE ART

OPPOSITE
48 **ANTHONY CARO**
Chair IV (After Van Gogh) 1997
Stoneware and rusted steel waxed
89 x 67 x 61 cm
LONDON, PRIVATE COLLECTION

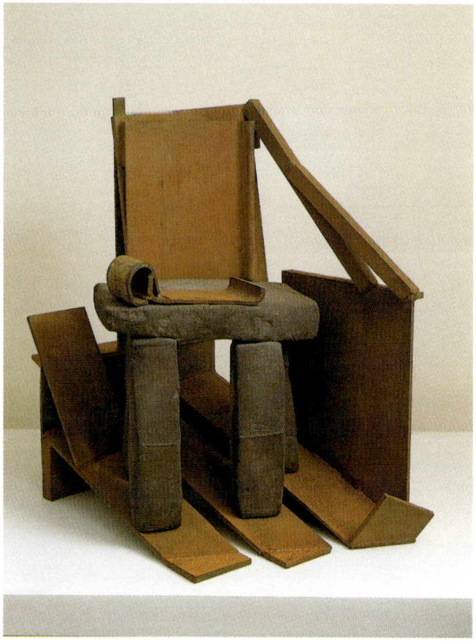

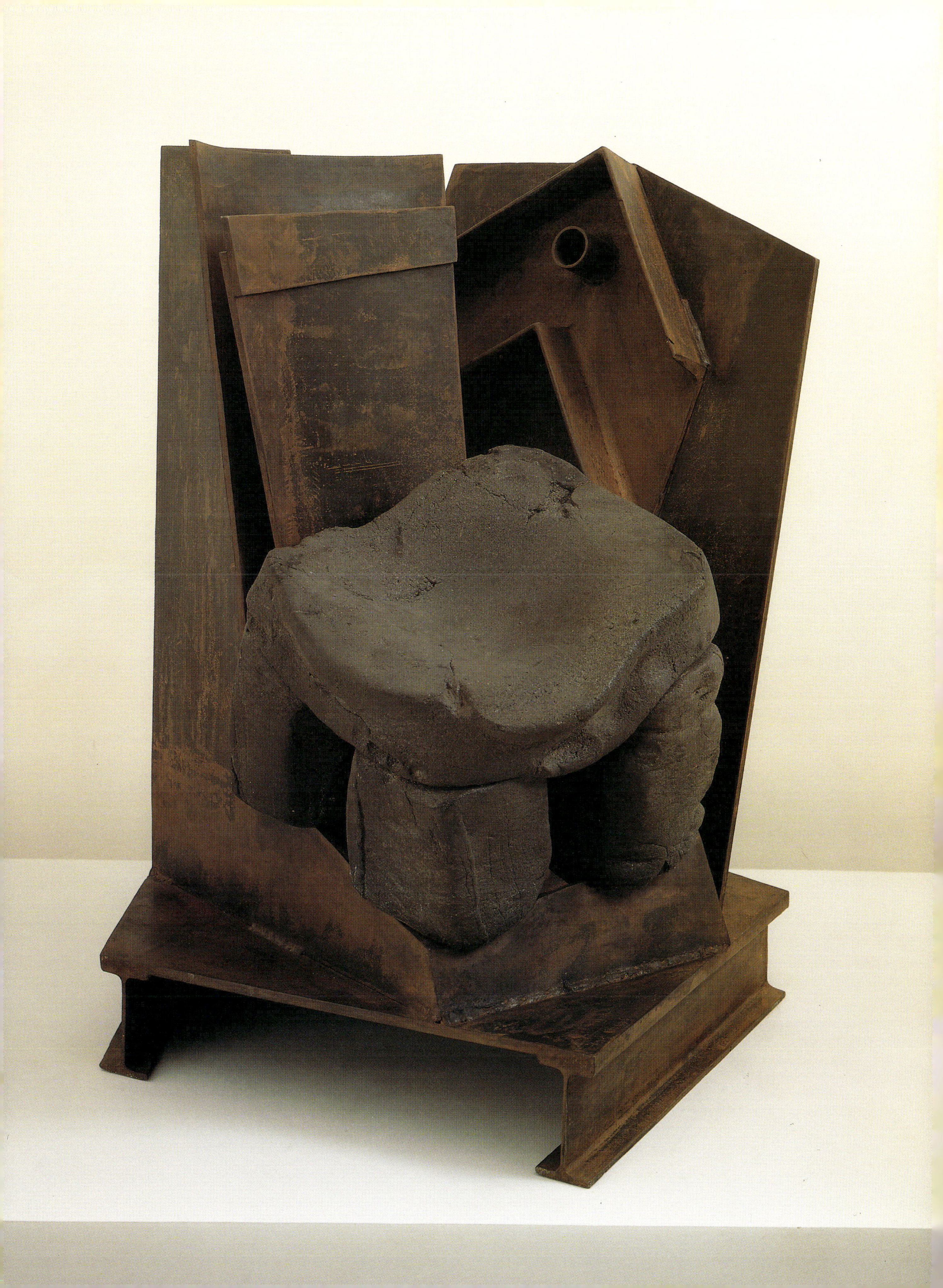

Van Gogh's own chair with its pendant, *Gauguin's Chair* (fig. 49), painted in December 1888, as a 'night effect'[18] – a premonition, perhaps, of the crisis which was to take place a few days later when the two men's working relationship reached its tragic climax.[19] Van Gogh returned to his own *Chair* after his release from hospital; he was to refer to its partner as 'Gauguin's empty place.'[20] Caro's *Chairs* (figs. 46, 47, and 48) declare themselves as such. The clay elements that stand in for rush-seating and legs were fashioned for the specific function they fulfil, although the clay was dropped, beaten (one might almost say bruised) to give it the vulnerability that it conveys within the context into which it is placed. The *Chairs* once again convey, very nakedly, Caro's ability to use abstract forms expressively. Whether they appear as swollen and lumpy or angular and fractured, they evoke a sense of psychological fragility. This feeling is enhanced by the way in which the *Chairs* also suggest the intimate but lonely interiors in which, in Van Gogh's originals, they are seen standing. The symbolic objects in the originals – a pipe, a tobacco pouch, a candle and two novels – are replaced by pieces of studio or industrial detritus.

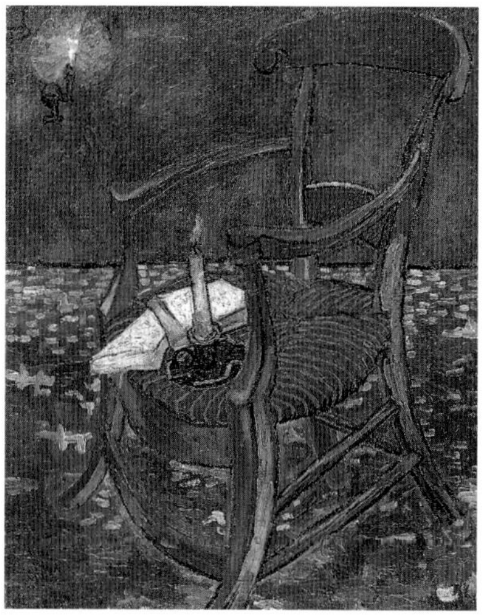

49 **VINCENT VAN GOGH**
Gauguin's Chair 1888
Oil on canvas
90.5 x 72.5 cm
AMSTERDAM, VAN GOGH MUSEUM

Table Piece, 'Dark Wood Beach' (1992–4: fig. 52) after Matisse's *Blue Nude ('Souvenir de Biskra')* (1907: fig. 50) and *Arena Piece, 'Beginning'* (1995: fig. 54), after Giotto's *Madonna in Majesty* (*c.*1306–10: fig. 53), are in sense complementary pieces in that they reflect opposing aspects of Caro's talent. During the course of many visits to the great Matisse exhibition mounted by New York's Museum of Modern Art in 1992, Caro found his attention increasingly arrested by the *Blue Nude*, possibly for the simple reason that it is the most sculptural of all Matisse's painted nudes. The painting had in fact been preceded by a related sculpture that had fallen apart, and immediately after finishing the picture Matisse produced another sculptural counterpart, *Reclining Nude (I), Aurora* (fig. 51). Caro's version provides us with a supreme example of his ability to put a flat, two-dimensional plane to sculptural purposes. Here, by its angling and because of the way it relates to the subsidiary forms around it, it stands in, with total conviction, for Matisse's fleshy, almost aggressively heavy female body. The shapes placed on the sculpture's 'table' or support, and the springy, plumelike configuration that replaces Matisse's palm fronds, relax the tensions contained in the main configurations to the left of them. This is a work of pure hedonism.

Arena Piece, 'Beginning', as its title suggests, commemorates another turning point in art: Giotto's *Madonna* was recognised from earliest times as an unaided and pivotal masterpiece from his hand. The way in which the dominant cone or egg shape in the sculpture reduces Giotto's mother and child to a single form suggests gestation, the beginning of life itself. For the first and only time in Caro's work there is an analogy with Brancusi's art, with those shapes with which the Romanian felt he could 'change the cosmos, make it to move otherwise.'[21] There is a sense in which the very use of wood somehow gets back to basics. This is one of the most reductive and the most solemn of all Caro's late sculptures. It conveys a sensation of centrality through subtle asymmetry. It is the first of the 'source' pieces to use colour, which here is simultaneously subdued but jewel-like. *'Beginning'* also gave birth to the *Arena* series inspired by scenes from Giotto's Arena Chapel in Padua. No one of these remarkable sculptures (which have yet to be seen in London) can be pinned down to a specific Giotto counterpart, although *Arena Piece, 'Visit'* (fig. 56) does bring irresistibly to mind the *Annunciation to Anna* (fig. 55). The series also unites Caro's passion for painting with his increasingly obsessive interest in architecture. In *Some Thoughts after Visiting Florence*, published in 1974, in which he linked the names of Donatello and Matisse, Caro wrote: 'The way in which architecture organised space made it the perfect tool for the Renaissance painter.'[22] Caro must surely already have been thinking about Giotto when he produced *Cathedral* (1988–91: fig. 57). He has said of it: 'I don't feel about my sculpture called *Cathedral* any different from what I feel about any sculpture I make. But it was about the idea of inwardness. And I think that's what gives it importance as a place. A place for and of itself, not a place for use or habitation just a pure place like a sculpture is itself only.'[23]

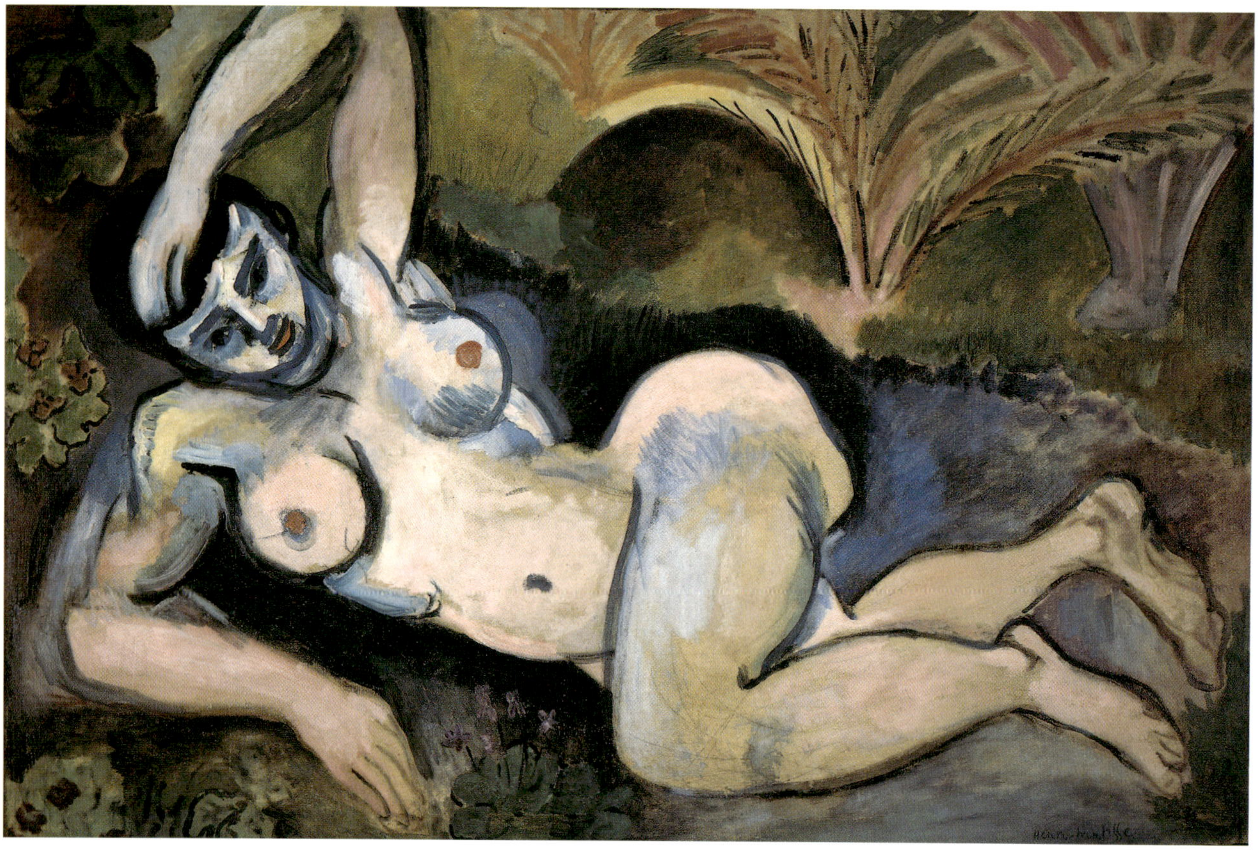

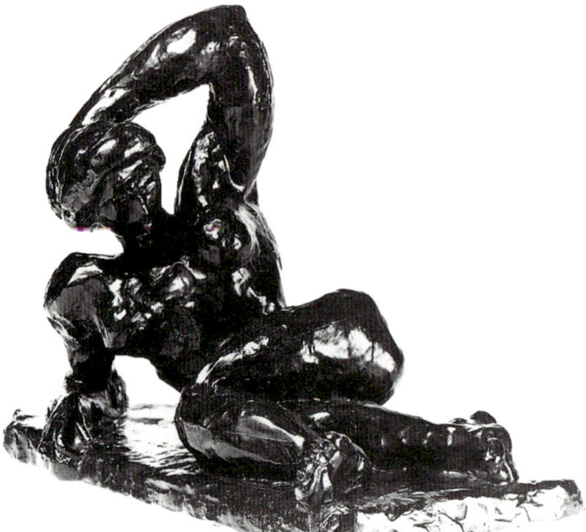

ABOVE

50 **HENRI MATISSE**

Blue Nude ('Souvenir de Biskra') 1907

Oil on canvas, 92.1 x 140.4 cm

THE BALTIMORE MUSEUM OF ART

LEFT

51 **HENRI MATISSE**

Reclining Nude (I), Aurora 1907

Bronze, 34.5 x 49.9 x 28 cm

THE BALTIMORE MUSEUM OF ART

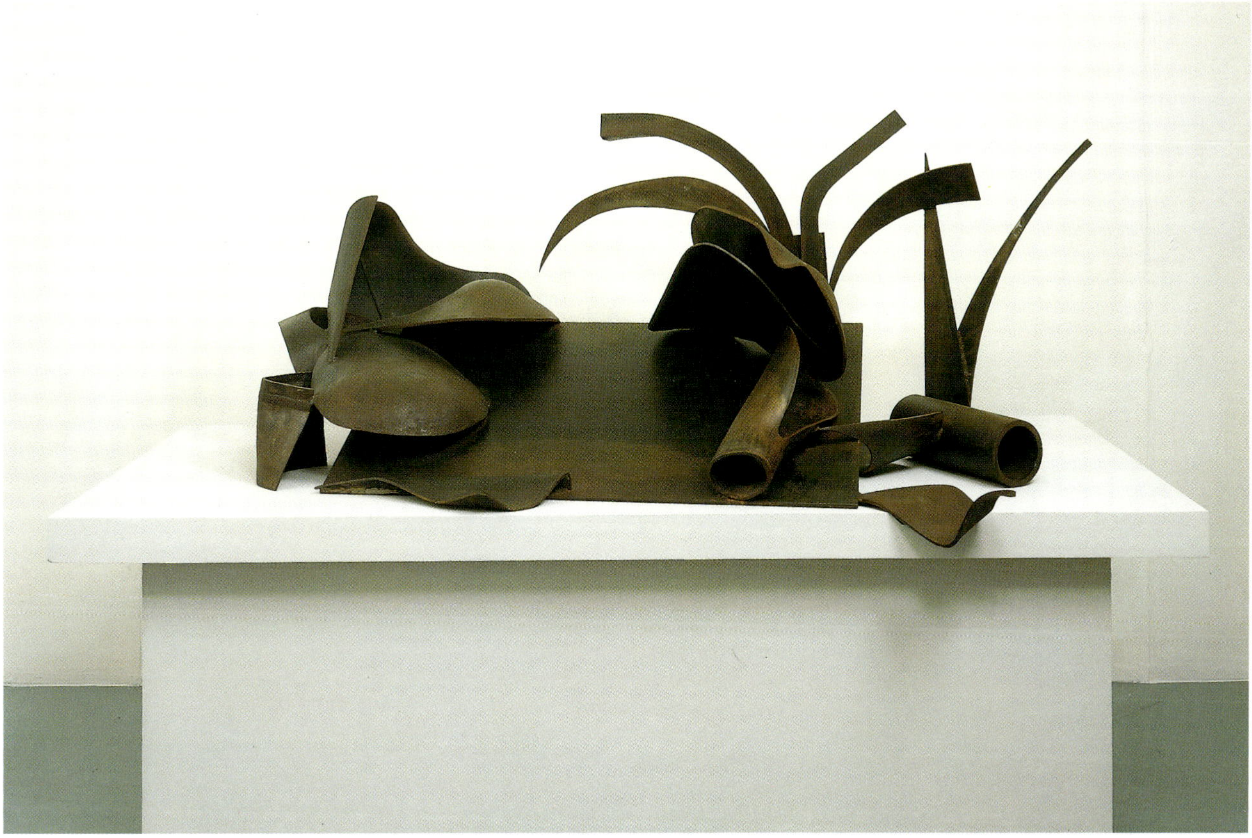

52 **ANTHONY CARO**
Table Piece, 'Dark Wood Beach' 1992–4
Steel waxed
77.5 x 155 x 103 cm
LONDON, PRIVATE COLLECTION

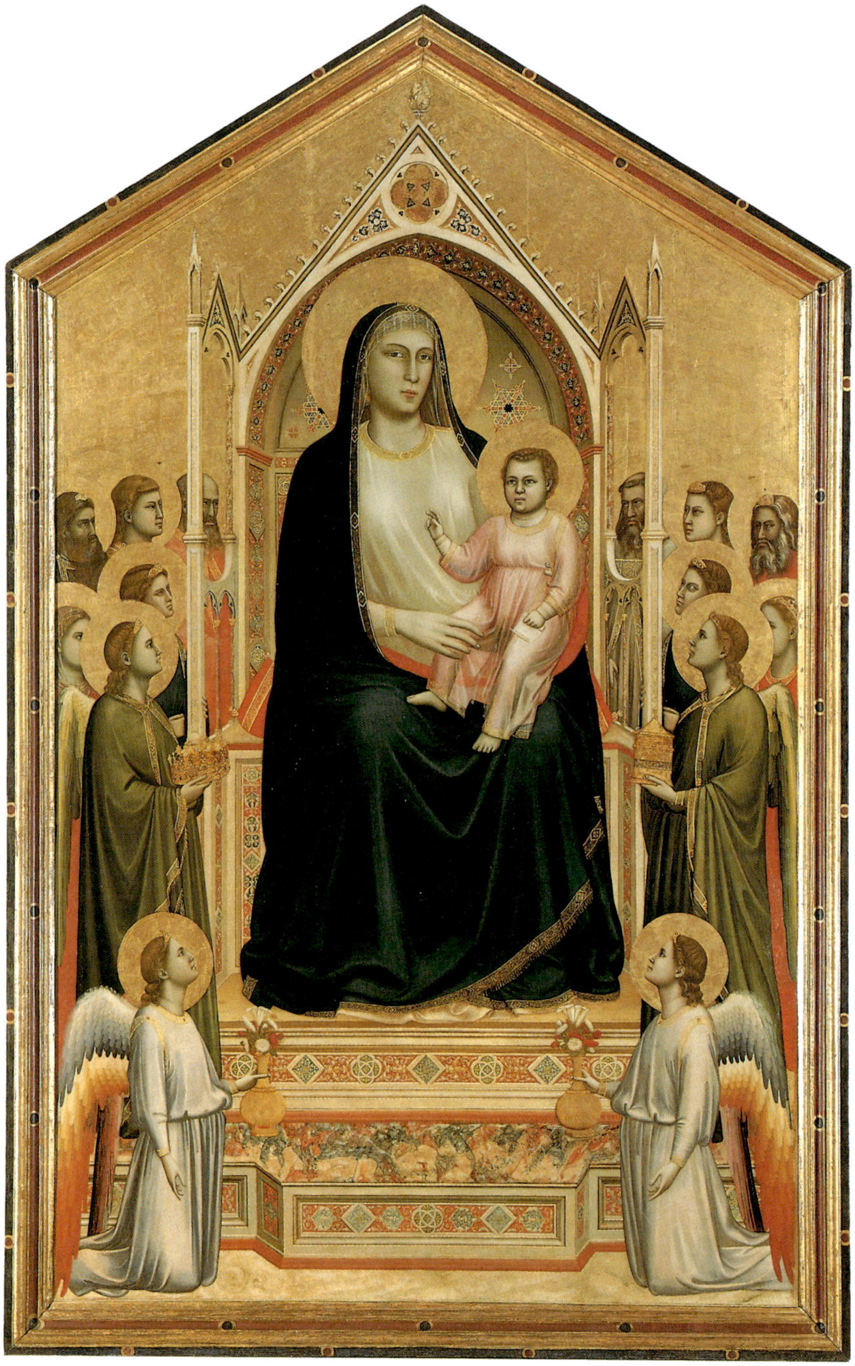

53 **GIOTTO**
Madonna in Majesty ('Ognissanti Madonna')
*c.*1306–10
Tempera on panel
325 x 204 cm
FLORENCE, GALLERIA DEGLI UFFIZI

54 **ANTHONY CARO**
Arena Piece, 'Beginning'
1995
Wood and steel painted
72 x 54 x 38 cm
LONDON, ANNELY JUDA FINE ART

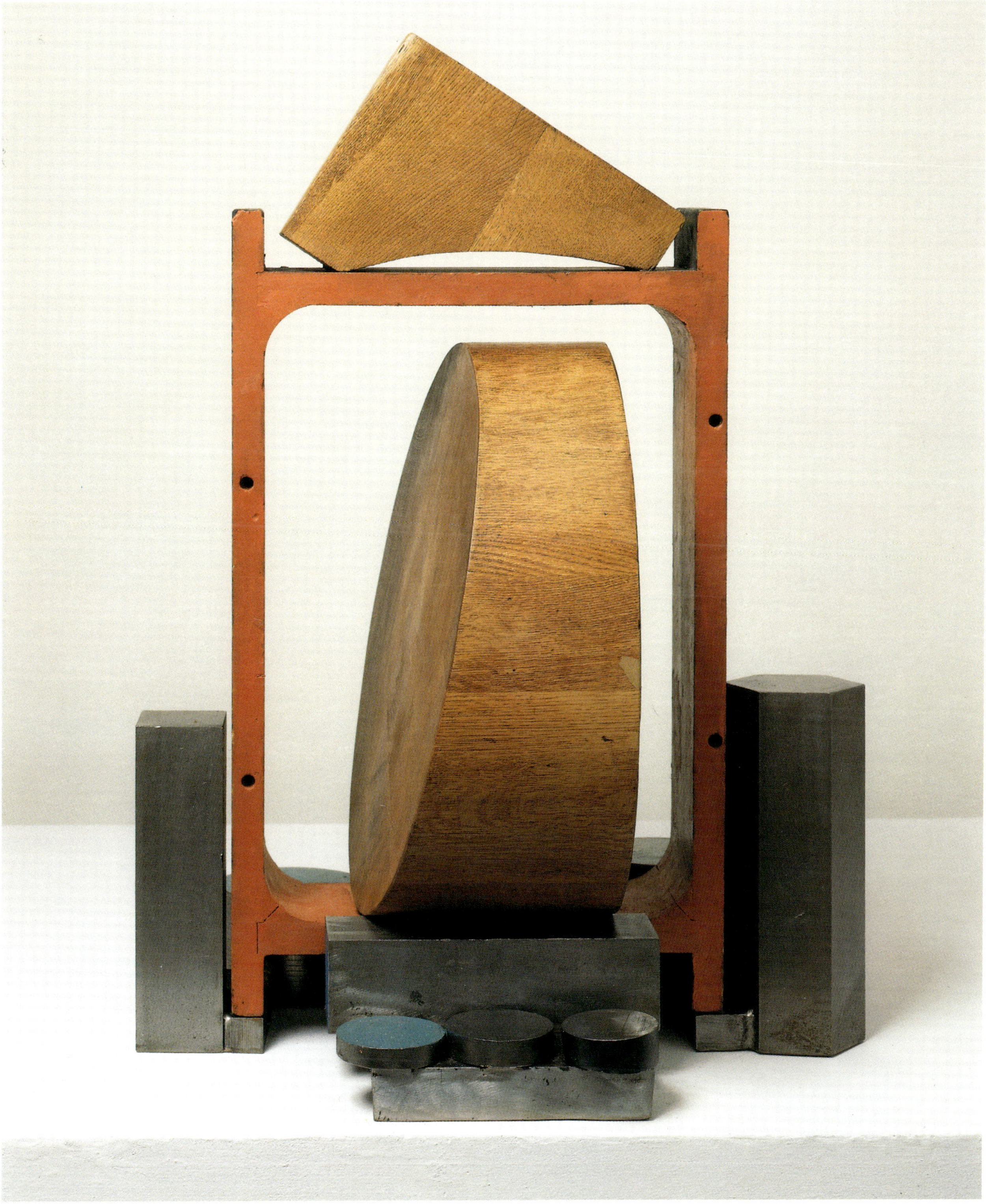

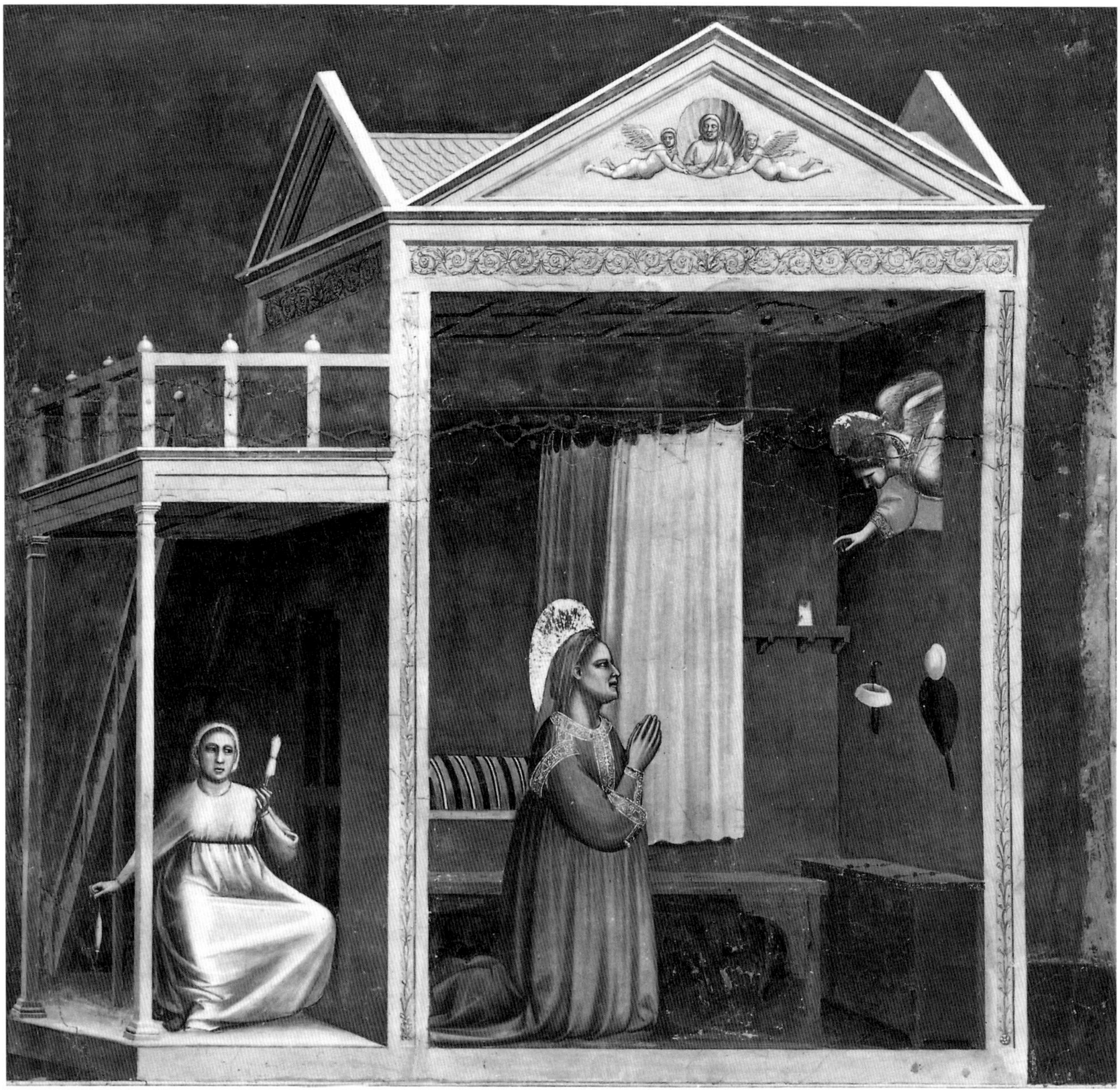

55 **GIOTTO**
Annunciation to Anna 1303–6
Fresco
185 x 200 cm
PADUA, CAPPELLA DEGLI SCROVEGNI ALL'ARENA

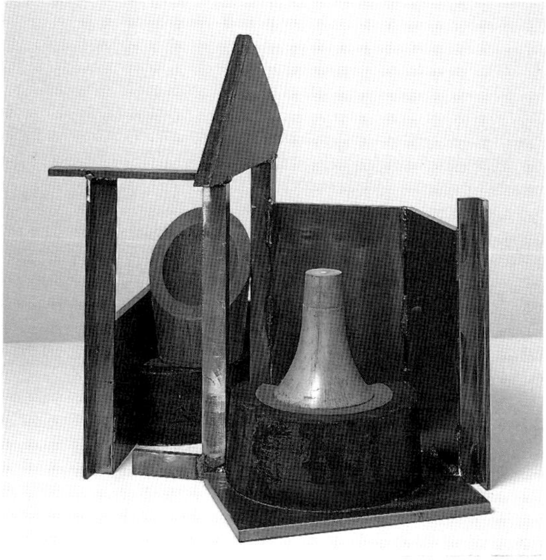

RIGHT
56 **ANTHONY CARO**
Arena Piece, 'Visit' 1995
Wood and steel painted
58 x 60 x 56 cm
LONDON, ANNELY JUDA FINE ART

BELOW
57 **ANTHONY CARO**
Cathedral 1988–91
Stainless steel, part painted
467.5 x 503 x 294.5 cm
LONDON, ANNELY JUDA FINE ART

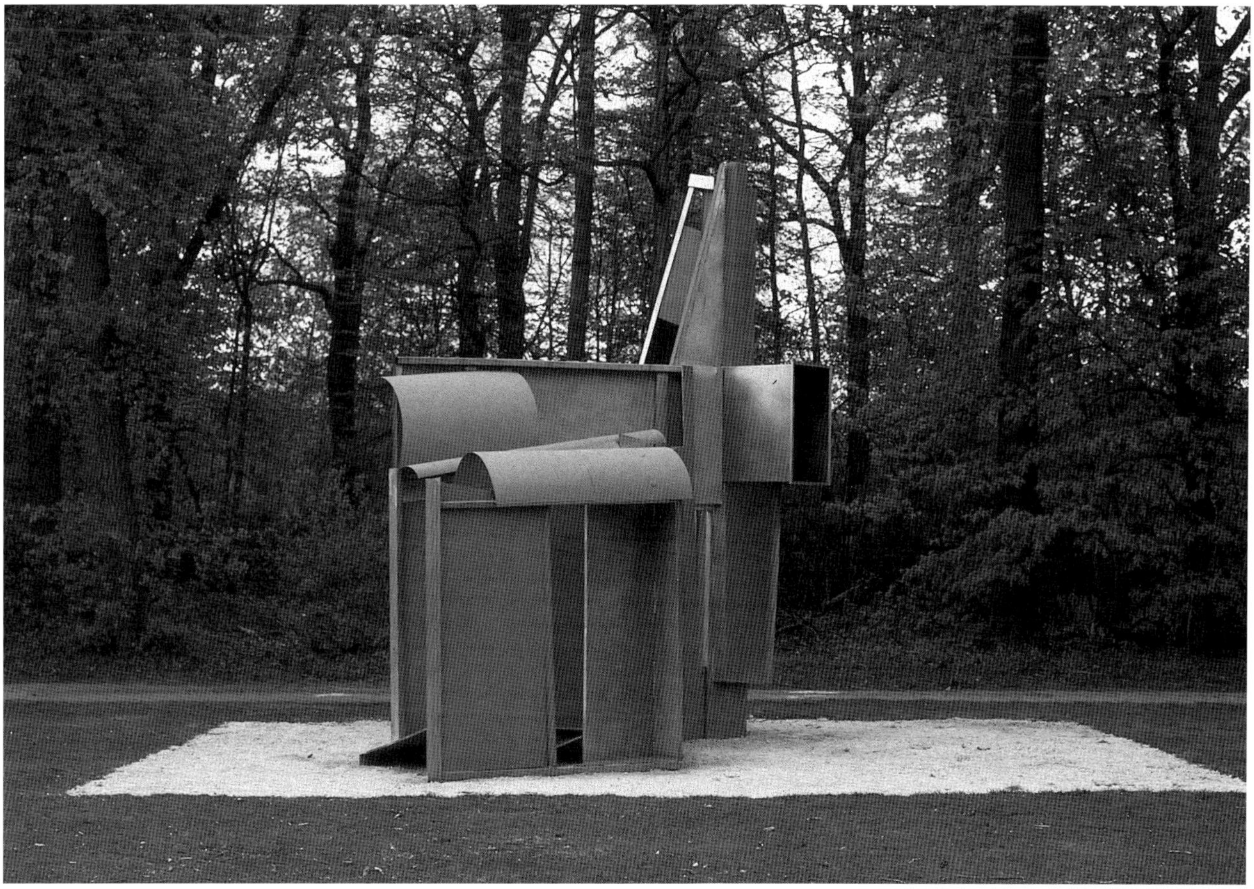

Notes

1. 'The Decline of Cubism', *Partisan Review*, March 1948.
2. 'Sculpture in Our Time', *Arts Magazine*, June 1939.
3. Quoted by Karen Wilkin in her essay 'Anthony Caro', *Caro*, Prestel 1991.
4. In conversation with the author, October 1997. This is a point Caro has made often before.
5. *The Artist's Eye, An Exhibition selected by Anthony Caro at The National Gallery, 1st June–24th July 1977*, Publications Department, National Gallery, London 1977. In this interview with Alastair Smith, Caro remarked, 'It was better to go to painting than to old sculpture because painting gave one ideas of what to do but no directions on how to do it.'
6. In conversation with the author, October 1997.
7. *Caro in Yorkshire*, The Henry Moore Sculpture Trust 1994. An interview with Robert Hopper, published on the occasion of Caro exhibitions held at the Henry Moore Studio, Dean Clough, Halifax, and the Yorkshire Sculpture Park, Wakefield, in the winter of 1994–5.
8. This point is also made in William Rubin, *Anthony Caro*, exh. cat., Museum of Modern Art, New York 1975, p. 169.
9. *After Olympia* is vast (332.5 x 2342 x 170 cm), and indeed approximates the size of the pediments of the Temple of Zeus itself. Caro prefers for it not to be viewed frontally, or head on, but rather in a large but not too wide space, as it was installed in 'Caro at The Trajan Markets' in Rome, 1992. It is now the property of E.P.A.D., La Défense, Paris, and is in an installation which, it can only be hoped, is temporary.
10. *Andrea Mantegna*, exh. cat., Royal Academy, London 1992, no. 116.
11. 'Modernist Painting', *Forum Lectures*, 1960.
12. Ibid.
13. *Picasso: Sculptor/Painter*, exh. cat., Tate Gallery, London 1994, pp. 37–8, 285–7.
14. Quoted in Diane Waldman, *Anthony Caro*, Cross River Press 1982, p. 25.
15. Disparate as Caro's sources may be, there are links that bind many of them together. Mantegna was one of the few Quattrocento painters in whom Rubens showed an interest. Rembrandt had studied Mantegna, and 'a precious book of Mantegna' was amongst his most treasured possessions. Degas, much admired by Caro as a sculptor, had copied Mantegna's work in the Louvre. Matisse and Picasso in very different ways had showed their veneration of Manet. Manet had in turn visually acknowledged his debt to Goya. Van Gogh was to influence Matisse in his early Fauve paintings and in old age Picasso was to become obsessed by Van Gogh.
16. Caro in conversation with David Sylvester and Robert Rosenblum at the time of the 1967 Picasso exhibition at the Tate, broadcast by the BBC in 1996 and published in 'Picasso as Sculptor', *Modern Painters*, Spring 1994.
17. Wilkin 1991 (cited in note 3).
18. *The Complete Letters of Vincent Van Gogh*, Thames & Hudson 1958, Vol. III, p. 108.
19. On 24 December 1888, Van Gogh's brother Theo received a telegram from Gauguin telling him that Vincent had severed a piece from one of his ears.
20. *Complete Letters* 1958 (cited in note 18), Vol. III, p. 256. Here the translation reads 'his empty chair'; but 'place' is more evocative of the original.
21. Quoted in Radu Varia, *Brancusi*, Rizzoli 1987, p. 15.
22. *Art International*, May 1974.
23. Quoted in Tim Marlow, *Anthony Caro*, exh. cat., Openluchtmuseum voor Beeldhouwkunst Middelheim, Antwerp 1997, pp. 65–6.

Select Chronology

1924
Born 8 March, New Malden, Surrey.

1937–42
Charterhouse School, Godalming, Surrey. During vacations works in studio of the sculptor Charles Wheeler.

1942–4
Christ's College, Cambridge; M.A. in engineering.
During vacations attends Farnham School of Art.

1944–6
Fleet Air Arm of Royal Navy.

1946–7
Regent Street Polytechnic, London: studies sculpture under Geoffrey Deeley.

1947–52
Royal Academy Schools, London.

1949
Marries the painter Sheila Girling (two sons Timothy, 1951, and Paul, 1958).

1951–3
Works as part-time assistant to Henry Moore.

1953–79
Teaches two days weekly at St Martin's School of Art, London.

1954
Moves to Hampstead; models figurative sculpture in clay and plaster.

1955
Included in group exhibition of sculpture, *New Painters and Painters-Sculptors*, at Institute of Contemporary Arts, London.

1956
First one-man exhibition, at Galleria del Naviglio, Milan.

1957
First one-man show in London, at Gimpel Fils Gallery.

1959
Wins sculpture prize at Paris Biennale.
Meets Clement Greenberg in London.
Visits USA for the fist time on Ford Foundation English Speaking Union Grant; meets Kenneth Noland and David Smith, also Robert Motherwell, Helen Frankenthaler and others.

1960
Returns to London; makes first abstract sculptures in steel including *Twenty Four Hours*.
Visits Carnac, Brittany, studies the menhirs and dolmens.

1961
First exhibits a steel sculpture, *The Horse*, 1961, in *New London Situation*, Marlborough New London Gallery, London.
First polychrome sculpture, *Sculpture Seven*.

1963
One-man exhibition of abstract steel sculptures at Whitechapel Gallery, London.

1963–5
Teaches at Bennington College, Bennington, Vermont.
Renews contact with Noland and Smith.

1964
First one-man exhibition in New York, at André Emmerich Gallery.

1965
Exhibits *Early One Morning*, 1962, in *British Sculpture in the Sixties*, Tate Gallery, London.

1966
Exhibits in *Five Young British Artists*, British Pavilion, Venice Biennale (with painters Richard Smith, Harold Cohen, Bernard Cohen and Robyn Denny).
Begins first table sculptures.

1967
Retrospective exhibition at Rijksmuseum Kröller-Müller, Otterlo.
Acquires stock of raw materials from estate of David Smith.

1968
Exhibits *Titan*, 1964, in *Noland, Louis and Caro*, Metropolitan Museum of Art, New York.

1969
Retrospective exhibition at Hayward Gallery, London.
Appointed Commander of the Order of the British Empire.
Exhibits, with John Hoyland, in British Section of Tenth São Paulo Biennale.
Patrick Cunningham becomes Caro's studio assistant.

1970
Begins making unpainted steel sculptures.

1971
Travels to Mexico, New Zealand, Australia and India.

1972
Makes sculptures using rolled steel at Ripamonte Factory, Veduggio, Brianza.

1973
One-man exhibition at Norfolk and Norwich Triennial Festival, East Anglia.
Museum of Modern Art, New York, acquires *Midday*, 1960.

1974
Works at York Steel Co., Toronto, and makes large sculptures, assisted by sculptors James Wolfe and Willard Beopple.

1975
Retrospective exhibition at Museum of Modern Art, New York (which later travels to Walker Art Center, Minneapolis Museum of Fine Art, Houston, and Museum of Fine Art, Boston).
Works in clay at workshop of Syracuse University, New York, organised by Margie Hughto.
Begins making sculptures in welded bronze.

1976
Presented with key to the City of New York by Mayor Abraham Beame.

1977
Exhibition of table sculptures at Tel Aviv Museum, later tours Australia, New Zealand and Germany.
Artist in residence at Emma Lake summer workshop, University of Saskatchewan.

1978
Makes first 'writing pieces': calligraphic sculptures in steel.
Executes commission for East Wing of the National Gallery, Washington.

1979
Receives Honorary Doctorates from East Anglia University, Norwich, and York University, Toronto.
Made Honorary Member of American Academy and Institute of Arts and Letters, New York.

1980
Makes first sculptures in lead and wood.

1981
Makes wall pieces in handmade paper, with Ken Tyler in New York.
Exhibits at Stadtische Galerie in Stadel, Frankfurt.
Made Honorary Fellow, Christ's College, Cambridge.

1982
Appointed Trustee of Tate Gallery, London.
Initiates Triangle annual summer workshops for sculptors and painters at Pine Plains, New York.
Joins Council of Slade School of Art, London

1984
One-man exhibition at Serpentine Gallery, London, which travels to Copenhagen, Düsseldorf and Barcelona. Creates first sculpture with an architectural dimension: *Child's Tower Room*.

1985
Visits Greece for the fist time.
Leads Sculptors' Workshop, Maastricht.
Receives Honorary Doctorate from Cambridge University.

1986
Completes work on *Scamander* and *Rape of the Sabines*, first of sculptures inspired by Greek pediments.
Made Honorary Fellow, Royal College of Art, London.

1987
Awarded knighthood, Queen's Birthday Honours.
Executes *After Olympia*, his largest sculpture.
Attends workshops in Berlin and Barcelona.

1988
Concludes investigation of pediment-inspired works with *Xanadu*.

1989
Exhibits at Walker Hill Art Center, Seoul.
Sculpture workshop, Edmonton.
Visits Korea and India.
Receives Honorary Degree, Yale University, New Haven.

1990
Exhibits at Musée des Beaux Arts, Calais.
Visits Japan and starts series of paper sculptures at Nagatani's workshop, Obama.

1991
Completes work on two large sculptures involving a dialogue with architecture: *Sea Music* for the quayside, Poole, Dorset, and *Tower of Discovery* for an exhibition of recent work at the Tate Gallery, London.

1992
Made Honorary Member, Accademia di Belle Arte di Brera.
Receives Praemium Imperiale award for sculpture, Tokyo.

1993–4
The British Council tours a selection of the *Cascades Series* of table pieces to museums in Hungary, Romania, Turkey, Cyprus and Greece.

1994
Receives Honorary Doctorate of the Royal College of Art, London.
Several exhibitions organised to celebrate the artist's 70th birthday, including: *The Trojan War*, shown at the Iveagh Bequest, Kenwood, London, and the Yorkshire Sculpture Park, Wakefield; *Sculpture Through Five Decades*, shown at Annely Juda Fine Art.

1994–5
Largest retrospective exhibition held at the Museum of Contemporary Art, Tokyo, curated by Yasuyoshi Saito with special architectural settings by Tadao Ando.
Exhibition of table sculptures organised by Kettle's Yard Gallery, Cambridge University, tours to Whitworth Art Gallery, University of Manchester, and Graves Art Gallery, Sheffield.
The Henry Moore Sculpture Trust commissions a temporary sculpture installation for the Henry Moore Studio at Dean Clough, Halifax: *Halifax Steps – Ziggurats and Spirals*.

1996
Receives Diploma Doctor Honoris Causa, University of Charles de Gaulle, Lille and Honorary Degree, Durham University.
Goodwood Steps displayed at the Hat Hill Sculpture Foundation, Goodwood.

1996–7
The *Trojan War* sculptures are shown in Greece at Thessaloniki and at the National Gallery, Athens.
With the architect Sir Norman Foster and the engineer Chris Wise, wins the competition for a new footbridge spanning the Thames from St Paul's to the new Tate Gallery of Modern Art at Bankside, London. Scheduled for completion in 2000, the bridge is known as the 'Millennium Bridge'.

To date Anthony Caro's sculpture is represented in the collections of 98 museums worldwide.

Lenders to the Exhibition

Creteil, Fonds départemental d'art contemporain, Conseil général du Val-de-Marne, France:
Descent from the Cross (After Rembrandt)

USA, Private Collection:
Table Piece Y-92, 'Triumph of Caesar'

London, Private Collection:
Chair IV (After Van Gogh)
Table Piece, 'Dark Wood Beach'
Table Piece Y-98, 'Déjeuner sur l'herbe II'

London, Annely Juda Fine Art:
Act of War (After Goya)
Arena Piece, 'Beginning'
Chair III (After Van Gogh)
Chair V (After Van Gogh)

Picture Credits

Amsterdam, Van Gogh Museum (Van Gogh Foundation): Figure 49

Baltimore, The Baltimore Museum of Art, The Cone Collection, formed by Dr Claribel Cone and Miss Etta Cone of Baltimore, Maryland BMA 1950.228: Figure 50; The Cone Collection, formed by Dr Claribel Cone and Miss Etta Cone of Baltimore, Maryland BMA 1950.429: Figure 51

Basel, Oeffentliche Kunstsammlung Basel, Kunstmuseum (Inv. no. 2261) (Photo: Martin Buhler): Figure 25

Belfast, Photograph reproduced by kind permission of the Trustees of the Ulster Museum, ©1959 Morris Louis: Figure 14

Brussels, Copyright IRPA-KIK: Figure 39

Chicago, Photograph © The Art Institute. All rights reserved. Charles H. and Mary F. S. Worcester Collection, 1953. 158: Figure 26

Florence, © Raffaello Bencini/Su concessione del Ministero per i Beni Culturali e Ambientali: Figure 53

London, Reproduced courtesy of Annely Juda Fine Art: Figures 1, 22 (Photos: Shigeo Anzai); Figure 4 (Photo: John Webb); Figure 8 (Photo: Guy Martin); Figure 15 (Photo: John Goldblatt); Figures 17, 27, 34, 38, 41, 43, 52, 54, 56 (Photos: John Riddy); Figure 24 (Photo: David Gooding); Figures 7, 9, 10, 12, 13, 19, 21, 28, 37, 46, 47, 48, 57

London, Reproduced by permission of the Henry Moore Foundation: Figures 2, 3

London, © British Museum: Figure 36

London, The Royal Collection © Her Majesty The Queen: Figures 20, 29, 30

Madrid, All rights reserved © Museo del Prado: Figure 42

New York, Photograph © 1997 The Museum of Modern Art. Gift of Walter P. Chrysler, Jr: Figure 18; Photograph © 1998 The Museum of Modern Art. Gift of Mr and Mrs Samuel A. Marx: Figure 23

New York, Reproduced by permission of the Artist: Figure 11

Padua, Musei Civici – Cappella Scrovegni: Figure 55

Paris, © Photo RMN: Figure 35

Peissenburg, Photograph by Blauel/Gnamm–ARTOTHEK: Figure 40

San Francisco, Museum of Modern Art, Gift of the Artist: Figure 16

© Estate of David Smith/VAGA, New York/DACS, 1998: Figure 5

© Kenneth Noland/VAGA, New York/DACS, 1998: Figure 6

© Succession H. Matisse/DACS, 1998: Figures 23, 26, 50, 51

© Succession Picasso/DACS, 1998: Figures 18, 25, 32, 33